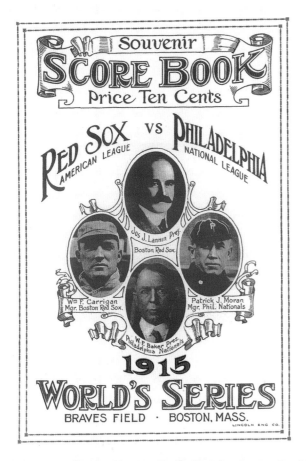

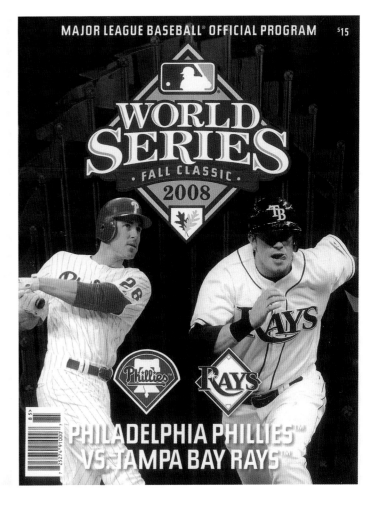

Philadelphia Phillies
Past & Present

Rich Westcott

MVP
BOOKS

Library of Congress Cataloging-in-Publication Data

Westcott, Rich.
  Philadelphia Phillies past & present / Rich Westcott.
     p. cm.
  Includes bibliographical references.
  ISBN 978-0-7603-3784-4 (hb w/ jkt)
  1. Philadelphia Phillies (Baseball team)--History. I. Title.
  GV875.P45W469 2010
  796.357'640974811--dc22
                                   2009028915

Edited by Josh Leventhal
Designed by Barbara Drewlo

Printed in China

On the front cover, top left: Gavvy Cravath, 1915 (Library of Congress, Prints and Photographs Division); *top right:* Mike Schmidt, 1987 (Stephen Dunn/Getty Images); *main image:* Phillies celebrate winning the National League Pennant, October 2009 (Chris McGrath/Getty Images).
On the title pages, main photo: Citizens Bank Park, October 2008 (Rob Tringali/Sportschrome/Getty Images); *inset photo:* Baker Bowl, circa 1920 (author's collection).
On the back cover, top left: Baker Bowl, 1916 (Transcendental Graphics/The Rucker Archive); *top right:* Citizens Bank Park, April 2009 (Ezra Shaw/Getty Images); *bottom left:* Deacon McGuire, 1887 (Library of Congress, Prints and Photographs Division); *bottom right:* Ryan Howard, 2009 (G Fiume/Getty Images).

Contents

PHILLIES PAST, PHILLIES PRESENT

By the time the Phillies were formed in 1883, baseball was already a well-established sport in Philadelphia. The game could be traced back to the early 1830s when club teams started appearing around the city. Within a few decades, more than 100 teams, including African-American teams, were playing baseball in the nation's first capital.

Philadelphia fielded a team, the Athletics, in the first professional league, the National Association of Professional Baseball Players, when it formed in 1871. Five years later, Philadelphia was the scene of the first National League game ever played. Then in 1882, another Philadelphia team, also known as the Athletics, was entered in the American Association when that league was established.

The Phillies' entry into the National League one year later resulted from the demise of two earlier franchises. The Syracuse Stars had entered the NL in 1879 but folded after one season. The Stars were replaced by a new team from Worcester, Massachusetts, called the Brown Stockings (or sometimes the Ruby Legs). When that team disbanded in 1882, a new and entirely unrelated franchise took its place in Philadelphia.

Al Reach—a former left-handed second baseman from England and one of baseball's first professional players as a member of a Philadelphia club called the Athletics in the mid-1860s—was asked by National League president A. G. Mills to start the new team. Having become a wealthy manufacturer and seller of sporting goods after retiring as a player in 1875, Reach readily accepted the challenge.

While putting together a team of mostly castoffs and minor league players and rebuilding a dilapidated old ballpark, Reach called his new club the Phillies because he thought the name would identify the team with the city where it played.

The Philadelphia Phillies made their debut on May 1, 1883, with a 4–3 loss to the Providence Grays. That might have been the high point of the season. The Phillies lost 13 of their first 17 games and went on to post a 17–81 record (.173), the worst in major league history, while finishing 46 games out of first place.

The following season, Reach hired Harry Wright to manage the club. Also born in England where he played cricket, Wright had become the premier manager in professional baseball. After piloting the Cincinnati Red Stockings as the first all-professional team in 1869, he later was the skipper of successful teams in Boston and Providence.

The Phillies' fortunes changed immediately. Under the astute Wright, the club began to improve so much that by 1885, it vaulted all the way to third place. The Phils jumped to second place in 1887. By the time Wright, headed for the Hall of Fame, retired after the 1891 season, his teams, except for his first year, had never finished lower than fourth in the standings.

Philadelphia Athletics vs. Brooklyn Atlantics, 1865

Philadelphia Phillies vs. Los Angeles Dodgers, 2009

By the beginning of the twentieth century, the Phillies had become one of the National League's most important franchises. And Philadelphia had fortified its place as a baseball hotbed and one of the country's foremost baseball cities.

Over more than 125 years, Phillies rosters have been graced with countless all-stars, Hall of Famers, and colorful characters. A cornerstone of the National League, the team experienced some extraordinary ups and downs, yet it continues to rate a special place in baseball history and in the hearts of generation after generation of Philadelphia baseball fans. Today, the Phillies have played longer in one city than every team except those in Chicago and Cincinnati. And the name "Phillies" is the longest continuous, one-city nickname in all of professional sports. A world championship in 2008 solidified the team's legacy in a new century.

TEAMS, RIVALS, LEAGUES

"The Phillies will meet the Indianapolis Hoosiers in a 3 p.m. game today at Philadelphia Base Ball Park."

Such a note might have appeared in a local newspaper in 1887. All the facts are right—but the Indianapolis Hoosiers? How could such a team be facing the Phillies?

For that matter, what's up with the Phils playing a team called the Detroit Wolverines? Or the Cleveland Spiders? Or the Brooklyn Bridegrooms?

All these teams—as well as the Pittsburgh Infants, Louisville Colonels, Baltimore Orioles, and others—at one time or another were members of the National League in the late 1800s and were regular opponents of the Phillies.

In that period, all kinds of teams with strange names performed in the National League. It was a league that changed teams—and size—regularly. Some franchises disbanded, others relocated, and still others simply changed their names, repeatedly.

When the Phillies first took the field in 1883, the National League consisted of 8 teams. The number expanded to 12 in 1892 when the league merged with the American Association and then went back to 8 in 1900. It stayed that way until 1961, when the addition of the New York Mets and Houston Colt .45s expanded the league to 10 teams.

When the Montreal Expos and San Diego Padres arrived in 1969, the league split into two six-team divisions, with the Phillies joining the Expos, Mets, Cardinals, Cubs, and Pirates in the National League East. In 1993, the Florida Marlins joined the East, and the Colorado Rockies were added to the West, until the league reorganized into three divisions the following year, placing the Phillies, Mets, Expos, Marlins, and Braves in the revamped East Division. Other than the Expos moving to Washington in 2005 to become the Washington Nationals, the Phillies' division mates have remained constant since 1994.

National League teams, 1888

Phillies manager Ben Chapman and Brooklyn Dodger Jackie Robinson, May 1947

Before the addition of new expansion teams, a few of the original National League clubs changed names or locations. The team from Brooklyn—known variably as the Bridegrooms, the Superbas, the Robins, the Trolley Dodgers, and finally just plain Dodgers—moved west to Los Angeles in 1958. During much of the club's time in Brooklyn, the Dodgers were the Phillies' biggest rival.

After the Dodgers won the pennant in 1920, they took a steady trip downward, eventually meeting the Phillies at the bottom of the barrel. Thereafter, the rivalry became particularly intense, with the two teams vying for the prize for most awful.

Usually, the Phillies earned the prize with a seventh- or eighth-place finish, while the Dodgers landed just ahead. Ironically, the only year that the Phils finished in the first division over a 31-year period was in 1932, when the team was managed by Burt Shotton. In the next decade, Shotton led Brooklyn to two pennants before he was ousted, which was in part caused by the Phillies winning the 1950 pennant at Ebbets Field on the last day of the season.

In the following years, especially after the Dodgers moved to Los Angeles, the rivalry cooled, although the teams did face off in consecutive League Championship Series in 1977 and 1978, with the Dodgers coming out on top both times. The Phillies won the next two LCS encounters, in 1983 and 2008.

In yet another strange twist of this long rivalry, between 1947 and 1992, three of the Dodgers' longest serving catchers (Roy Campanella, Mike Sciosia, and Mike Piazza) were natives of the Philadelphia area.

Phillies and Dodgers scuffle at Dodger Stadium, 2008 NLCS

Mike Schmidt fights Bruce Kison of the Pittsburgh Pirates, July 1977

There was a time, especially in the 1970s, when the Phils had a strong rivalry with the Pittsburgh Pirates—and not only because the teams were from the same state. The two were annually among the top teams in the NL East Division, and from 1975 to 1978 they ranked one-and-two, with the Phillies winning three division titles in that span. The teams constantly challenged each other on the field, sometimes leading to fights or near fights. From the standpoint of the home fans, no opponent was more disliked than Pittsburgh.

That view was replaced in later years by an even greater aversion to the New York Mets. It was a case of not only the teams but also their fans intensely disliking each other.

There has, of course, always been a strong rivalry between the cities of New York and Philadelphia, and in a way, baseball served as an extension of that animosity. In recent years, however, when the teams have been among the leaders of their division, the mutual distaste has heightened.

The tension gained momentum in 2007 when Phils shortstop Jimmy Rollins, on his way to becoming the league's Most Valuable Player, boasted that his club was the "team to beat" in the East Division. Other comments flew back and forth from players on both squads, but Rollins' prediction ultimately proved true. Then, amid more acerbic comments in 2008, the rivalry intensified. Today, no rivalry is more bitter than the one between the Phils and the Mets.

The Phillies have had one other long-term rival in their history—the Philadelphia Athletics of the American League. From 1901 through 1954, the teams shared a city, and from mid-1938 on, they shared a ballpark too. In most years starting in 1903, the teams also met in a widely anticipated City Series.

Each team had its loyal fans, and the relative merits of the clubs were an often and loudly debated subject. Through much of that time, with the A's having won nine pennants to the Phillies' two, the American Leaguers were more popular. That condition began to abate, however, as the post–World War II Phillies started fielding good teams while the Athletics slipped steadily downhill. When the Whiz Kids won the pennant in 1950, large numbers of fans swung over to the Phils' side. Fielding mostly losing teams and attracting tiny crowds, the Athletics' long residence in Philadelphia ended a few years later, when they moved to Kansas City after the 1954 season.

Phillies and Mets brawl at Shea Stadium, August 1990

Jimmy Rollins collides with Carlos Beltran of the New York Mets, April 2007

PHILLIE FIRSTS

As a city that founded a nation, Philadelphia has had a role in many notable baseball firsts.

Through the first 60 years of organized professional leagues, it was generally agreed that professional baseball was not a game to be played at night. Cincinnati Reds general manager Larry MacPhail had another idea, however. He knew that some minor league, Negro League, and amateur teams on occasion had played under lights, so why couldn't big league teams?

So, MacPhail had lights installed at Cincinnati's Crosley Field, and on May 24, 1935, the Reds played host to the Phillies in the first major league night game. The Phillies were perennial losers at the time, so the game itself was not a big draw, but the feebleness of the Reds' opponent was overshadowed by the novelty of the event. A crowd of 20,422 was on hand for the landmark game.

From the White House in Washington, President Franklin D. Roosevelt pulled a switch to turn on the Crosley Field lights, and the game began. Cincinnati's Paul Derringer allowed six hits in the 2–1 victory, while Philadelphia's Joe Bowman yielded just four hits in a losing effort.

Fourteen years earlier, the Phils had participated in another pioneering event: the first radio broadcast of a big league baseball game. The Phillies–Pirates contest on August 5, 1921, was aired in Pittsburgh on station KDKA with Harold Arlin handling the play-by-play. (Arlin was the grandfather of Steve Arlin, a one-time Phillies bonus baby in the late 1960s.)

The Phillies also were participants in the first official major league game played indoors, when they met the Houston Astros in the Astrodome's regular-season debut on April 12, 1965, and they played in the first official game on foreign soil, defeating the Expos in the opener of Montreal's Olympic Stadium on April 15, 1977.

Woodrow Wilson, 1915 World Series

On their home turf, the Phillies' Baker Bowl, originally called Philadelphia Base Ball Park, was the first ballpark built with bricks. In 1915, Woodrow Wilson became the first U.S. president to attend a World Series game when he visited Baker Bowl on October 8. In 1933, the Phillies were the first team to enact a knot-hole gang, offering free admission to kids who had watched games through holes in the outfield wall at Baker Bowl. The first woman to hold a full-time scouting job with a big league team was Edith Houghton, who spent seven years with the Phillies starting in 1946.

Among other individual firsts, the first major leaguer killed in World War I was former Phillies third baseman Eddie Grant, then a member of the New York Giants. The first big league player to enter the military in World War II was Phillies pitcher Hugh Mulcahy, who was called to arms in 1941.

In the 1890s, Philadelphia's Roy Thomas became the first player to protect his hands by wearing gloves for sliding headfirst into bases. Many decades later, Phils catcher Bob Boone was the middle part—following dad Ray and preceding sons Bret and Aaron—of the first three-generation family to play in the majors.

Phillies center fielder Billy Hamilton became the first major leaguer to score more than 180 runs in one season, when he crossed the plate 192 times in 1894. In 1942, left fielder Danny Litwhiler became the first outfielder to play in at least 150 games during one season without committing an error. In 1950, Jim Konstanty became the first relief pitcher to win the Most Valuable Player Award.

The first perfect game hurled in the National League after the pitching mound was moved to a distance of 60 feet, 6 inches from home plate was tossed in 1964 by the Phillies' Jim Bunning against the New York Mets. Juan Samuel was the first major league player to reach double figures in doubles, triples, home runs, and stolen bases in each of his first four seasons (1984–1987).

One first that the Phillies would just as soon forget was achieved in 2007, when the club became the first professional sports team to lose 10,000 games. They did it with a 10–2 loss to the St. Louis Cardinals on July 15 during what was, ironically, the first season in 14 that the Phils reached the postseason. The Phillies' total was more than 300 losses ahead of the second-place Boston-Milwaukee-Atlanta Braves and more than 500 losses worse than the Chicago Cubs, both teams that began in 1876. At the time of their historic loss, the Phillies had accumulated 8,810 wins.

Edith Houghton, late 1940s

Fan holding sign for Phillies 10,000th loss, July 2007

Pennants and World Series

Despite having been around longer than most franchises, the Phillies have not ventured often to the Fall Classic compared to some teams. But when they have, especially when they win, the city of Philadelphia has turned into a place that even the redoubtable Billy Penn wouldn't recognize.

A notable recent example occurred in 2008 when the Phillies won a memorable five-game set against the Tampa Bay Rays. It was only the second World Series victory for the Phillies, but like the first one in 1980, it turned the city upside down.

The first time the Phillies reached the World Series was in 1915, when a team led by 31-game-winner Grover Cleveland Alexander and National League home run and RBI champ Gavvy Cravath finished in first place with a seven-game lead. The World Series against the Boston Red Sox that October had a far different result, however. Manager Pat Moran's Phils won the opener behind Alexander but then went on to lose three straight by 2–1 scores before dropping the finale, 5–4.

Phillies manager Pat Moran and Red Sox manager Bill Carrigan confer with umpires prior to 1915 World Series

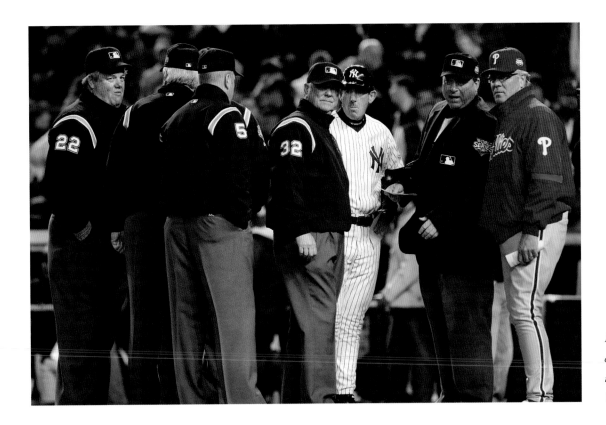

Phillies and Yankees coaches confer with umpires prior to 2009 World Series

Tug McGraw, World Series Game Six, October 21, 1980

Brad Lidge, World Series Game Five, October 29, 2008

It was 35 years before the Phillies won another pennant. This time, a team nicknamed the Whiz Kids because of a roster loaded with young players—including Richie Ashburn, Del Ennis, Willie Jones, and Granny Hamner and pitchers Robin Roberts and Curt Simmons—held a 7-game lead with 11 games remaining. Losses in seven of their next nine games left the Phillies with just a two-game lead as they headed into a two-game series on the final weekend against the second-place Brooklyn Dodgers. The Phils lost the first game, 7–3.

That Sunday, with Ebbets Field crammed to the rafters and the score tied 1–1 in the bottom of the ninth, Ashburn threw out Cal Abrams at the plate to stave off a Dodger victory.

Then, in the top of the 10th, delivering the biggest hit in Phillies history, Dick Sisler clubbed a three-run homer to give his team a 4–1 lead. Roberts, making his third start in six days, polished off Brooklyn in the bottom half of the inning to secure his first 20-win season and send the Phillies to the World Series.

For the Fightin' Phils, as they were also known, the 1950 World Series was anticlimactic. Facing the powerful New York Yankees, the Phils lost the opener, 1–0, when, because of an exhausted starting rotation, manager Eddie Sawyer was forced to start reliever Jim Konstanty, who would later be named the National League's MVP. Two more one-run losses followed before the Phillies finally succumbed, 5–2, in the fourth game.

Garry Maddox carried off the field after clinching the pennant, NLCS Game Five, October 12, 1980

The Whiz Kids celebrate after clinching the pennant, October 1, 1950

Another 30 years would pass before the Phillies next visited the World Series. This time, having lost in the NLCS in three of the previous four years, the Phils won the NL East Division title in 1980 by one game, with Cy Young Award winner Steve Carlton posting 24 wins and MVP Mike Schmidt leading the league in home runs and runs batted in.

In what many regard as one of the most memorable postseason battles in baseball history, the Phillies overcame a two-games-to-one deficit to beat the Houston Astros in the NLCS and win the pennant. After three of the first four games went into extra innings, the Phils rallied for five runs in the eighth inning of Game Five, with Houston's Nolan Ryan on the mound, to take a 7–5 lead. Houston came back to score twice in the bottom of the inning to tie the game and send it into overtime. Garry Maddox's tenth-inning double drove home the winning run to give the Phillies a pennant-clinching 8–7 victory.

Manager Dallas Green's club continued its heroics in the World Series against the Kansas City Royals, winning the first

Above: *Mitch Williams and Darren Daulton celebrate clinching the pennant, NLCS Game Six, October 13, 1993*

Left: *Mike Schmidt and Al Holland celebrate clinching the pennant, NLCS Game Four, October 8, 1983*

two games at home. The Royals pulled even, but the Phils won the last two games, clinching the Series in Game Six with a 4–1 victory behind the pitching of Carlton and reliever Tug McGraw. After Pete Rose caught a foul pop that had bounced off the glove of catcher Bob Boone, McGraw fanned Willie Wilson to end the game. The first World Series triumph in Phillies history touched off a momentous celebration in Philadelphia.

The Phillies won another World Series berth in 1983 after cruising to the division title by six games. Led by Cy Young winner John Denny and home run king Schmidt, the team was nicknamed the Wheeze Kids because of a lineup heavily stocked with veteran players, including Rose, Joe Morgan, and Tony Perez. With Gary Matthews leading the attack and earning the series MVP Award, the Phillies took three of four from the Los Angeles Dodgers to win the NL pennant.

Under Paul Owens, who near midseason had moved from general manager to manager, the Phillies faced the Baltimore Orioles in the 1983 World Series. Denny won the opener, but the Orioles took the next four games, two by one run, to capture the crown.

In 1993, a year after finishing in last place, the Phillies won 97 games to capture the division crown by three games. Sitting in the back of the clubhouse in what was known as Macho Row, Darren Daulton presided over an earthy band of scruffies that he called gypsies, tramps, and thieves—foremost among them being John Kruk and Lenny Dykstra. In the NLCS, the Phils were heavy underdogs to the Atlanta Braves, but with reliever Mitch Williams recording one win and three saves, manager Jim Fregosi's club won four of six games for a hard-earned pennant.

In the World Series, the Phillies performed admirably against the powerful Toronto Blue Jays. After a disheartening 15–14 loss in Game Four—a 4-hour, 14-minute affair—the Phils came back the next day to win, 2–0, on Curt Schilling's five-hitter. The party ended, though, in the sixth game when

Ryan Howard homers, World Series Game Four, October 26, 2008

Joe Carter's three-run homer in the bottom of the ninth off Williams gave the Blue Jays an 8–6 victory and the Series. Afterward, Fregosi was roundly criticized for putting the battle-weary Williams into the game.

It would be another 15 years before the Phillies found their way back to the Fall Classic. But as Phillies fans will readily admit, the wait was worth it.

The climax of the 2008 championship was a parade to end all parades, with the entire team perched on the backs of trucks and riding four miles from center city to Citizens Bank Park. An estimated 2.5 million fans jammed the parade route, many of them following the procession down Broad Street to a rally that needed two stadiums to hold all the people.

The celebration put the finishing touches on a remarkable season in which the Phillies, despite holding or sharing first place for all but six days between June 1 and August 13, had to stage a monumental late-season rally to capture the East Division title. Down by 3½ games on September 10, the Phils won 13 of their last 16, while the New York Mets staged their second straight season-ending collapse and lost 9 of their final 15 games.

Manager Charlie Manuel, in his fourth season at the helm, not only became one of the city's most popular figures, but he adroitly ran a team that stole the hearts of baseball fans throughout

World Series victory parade on Broad Street, October 31, 2008

the Philadelphia area. In fact, the Phils attracted a club-record 3,422,583 fans during the season, including 50 sellouts.

The Phillies erased the Milwaukee Brewers in four games in the National League Division Series, with Shane Victorino's grand slam and Pat Burrell's two homers rating special headlines. The Phils won the pennant by defeating the Dodgers in five games in the National League Championship Series. Matt Stairs' pinch-hit homer in Game Four, NLCS MVP Cole Hamels' two wins, and Brad Lidge's three saves led the way.

In the World Series, the Phillies needed just five games to dispatch of the Tampa Bay Rays, capturing three of their four wins by one run. One game ended at 1:47 a.m. after a long rain delay, and the clincher began one day and—after another rain delay halted the game in the sixth inning—ended two days later when the final three and a half innings were staged after the resumption of play. Ryan Howard homered three times and drove in six runs in the series; Lidge saved two more games, including the clincher;

and Hamels pitched brilliantly in Games One and Five to earn Series Most Valuable Player honors.

The 2008 champs were an enormously likeable group that could legitimately lay claim to being the most popular team in Philadelphia sports history. Indeed, no Philadelphia team had won a championship in 25 years (since the 76ers in 1983) before the Phillies returned the city to glory.

A year later, with just a few tweaks to the roster, the Phils entered their second straight World Series for the first time in franchise history. The defending champs clinched the pennant by again besting the Dodgers in five games in the NLCS. It was a different story in the World Series, though, as the Phillies fell to the New York Yankees, four games to two, in a skirmish between representatives of the East Coast's two largest cities. Despite the loss, the Phils made a commendable showing, led by Chase Utley's record-tying five World Series home runs and newcomer Cliff Lee's two wins on the mound.

1887 Philadelphia Phillies

OTHER GREAT TEAMS

Along with the seven World Series teams, the Phillies have fielded other exceptional clubs over the years. They have not been abundant, but they have given the franchise, especially in the last four decades, a much more respectable position in the baseball pantheon than it had in most of its previous eight decades.

Excellent Phillies teams first appeared in the late 1880s, and from 1886 through 1895, they never finished lower than fourth place in the standings. Under the guidance of Harry Wright, the 1886 Phils finished with 71 wins and 43 losses (and 5 ties) for a .623 win-loss percentage—the best by any Phillies team for the next 90 years—but ended up in fourth place. A year later, the team finished second, just three and a half games out, which was the closest they would get to the top until the 1915 pennant season. The 1894 Phils finished fourth despite scoring a franchise-record 1,143 runs and batting .349 as a team.

By the end of the nineteenth century, numerous top players had worn the Phillies uniform, including future Hall of Famers Ed Delahanty, Sam Thompson, Billy Hamilton, Nap Lajoie, and Elmer Flick. Pitcher Charlie Ferguson, who won 99 games in four seasons; Kid Gleason, a 38-game winner in 1890; and Jack Clements, a left-handed catcher who spent nearly 14 seasons with the Phils, were among other standouts.

Closing out the century, the 1899 Phils finished third with a record of 94–58–2 under manager Billy Shettsline. The roster featured three 20-game winners in Red Donahue, Chick Fraser, and Wiley Piatt, while Delahanty (.410), Lajoie (.378), Flick (.342), and Roy Thomas (.325) spearheaded a potent lineup. No Phillies team would win as many games until the 1976 club won 101.

The 1913 team managed by Red Dooin placed second with an 88–63 record, 12½ games out of first. Then, after winning the pennant in 1915, the Phils finished second with 91–62 and 87–65

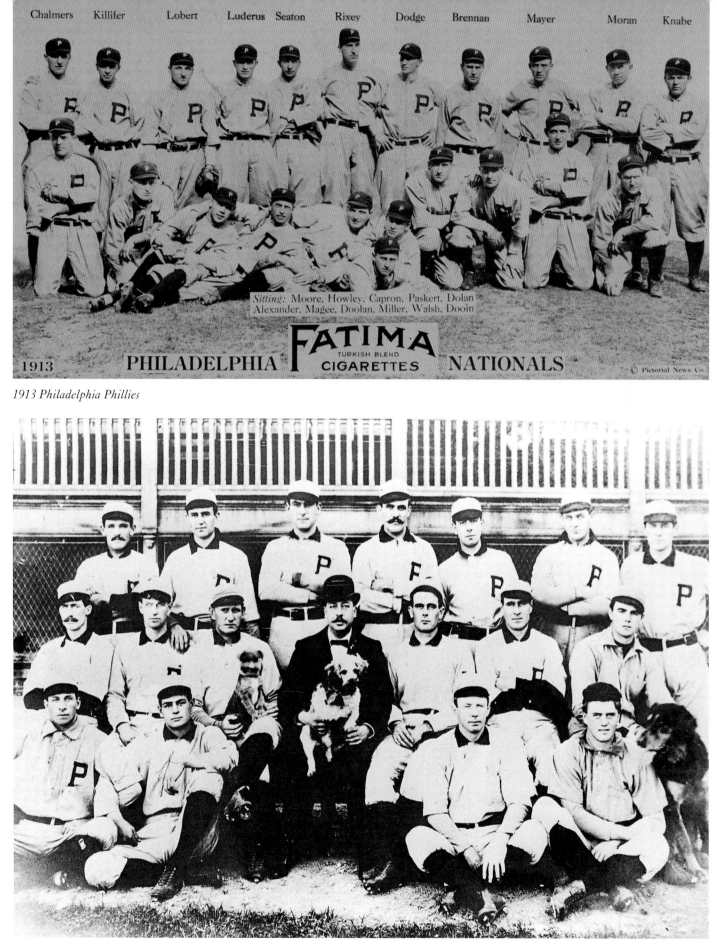

Sitting: Moore, Howley, Capron, Paskert, Dolan
Alexander, Magee, Doolan, Miller, Walsh, Dooin

FATIMA
TURKISH BLEND
CIGARETTES

1913   PHILADELPHIA   NATIONALS

© Pictorial News Co.

1913 Philadelphia Phillies

1899 Philadelphia Phillies

marks in the next two years before owner William Baker began unloading his top players, most notably Grover Cleveland Alexander.

The Phillies didn't have another winner until 1950, and quickly thereafter they returned to also-ran status. They retained that status—except for the year of the great collapse, 1964—until the mid-1970s.

In the period known as the Golden Era, from 1975 to 1983, the Phils won five East Division titles, two National League pennants, and one World Series. The club finished in second place in two other seasons during that nine-year stretch and never had a losing season.

Led by future Hall of Famers Mike Schmidt and Steve Carlton and standout stars such as Greg Luzinski, Garry Maddox, Larry Bowa, Bob Boone, and Tug McGraw, the Phils won a club-record 101 games in both 1976 and 1977. In those years and in 1978, manager Danny Ozark's teams won the division and advanced to the League Championship Series, only to get swept by the Cincinnati Reds in 1976 and then fall to the Los Angeles Dodgers in each of the next two years.

The 1977 NLCS was particularly painful and remains a sore spot in Phillies history. In the third game, on what would become known as "Black Friday," Ozark neglected to replace left fielder Greg Luzinski with Jerry Martin, a far superior defensive player. In the top of the ninth inning with the Phils leading 5–3, Luzinski failed to catch a ball hit to deep left by Manny Mota that Martin would've easily grabbed, and with the aid of a blown call at first by umpire Bruce Froemming, the Dodgers scored three runs to capture a 6–5 victory and take a two-games-to-one lead in the series. One night later, in pouring rain, the Phillies lost to Tommy John and the Dodgers, 4–1, in a bitter end to the series.

Larry Bowa and teammates celebrate clinching the division, September 28, 1977

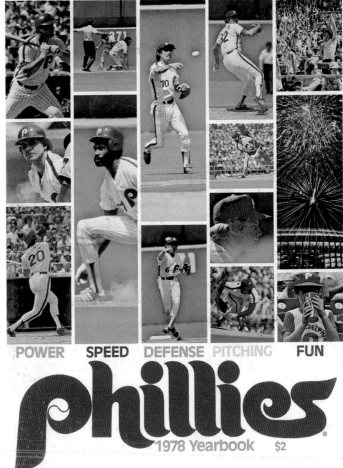

Phillies yearbook, 1978

Nonetheless, the 1977 team is often called the best in Phillies history. With the group above, plus Larry Christenson, Bake McBride, Jay Johnstone, and Richie Hebner also playing key roles, the club finished five games ahead of the Pittsburgh Pirates while leading the league in batting average and runs scored.

A year after winning the World Series in 1980, the Phils made the playoffs in the strike-shortened, split season of 1981. After being declared the first-half winners, they were eliminated by the Montreal Expos, three games to two, in a special playoff to decide the East Division champion.

Following six straight sub-.500 seasons, the Phillies returned to the top in 1993, but the time among the elite was short, with seven more losing seasons to follow. A winning streak returned in the new century under managers Larry Bowa and Charlie Manuel. Between 2001 and 2009, the Phils never finished below third place in the East and lost more games than they won only once (80–81 in 2002).

The 2007 team, led by MVP Jimmy Rollins, was the first one since 1993 to reach the playoffs. Winning 13 of their last 17 regular-season games while the New York Mets lost 12 of 17, the Phillies reached the League Division Series only to lose in three straight to the Colorado Rockies.

The 2009 division title was the tenth time the Phillies have appeared in postseason play since the creation of divisions in 1969.

Manager Charlie Manuel (center) and team celebrate clinching the division, September 30, 2007

LOSERS

itcher/philosopher Curt Schilling once said that "losing is the only way to grasp the true meaning of winning." If that's true, the Phillies have had ample opportunity to prepare.

Although the first decade of the twenty-first century produced eight winning seasons, three division titles, and a world championship in Philadelphia, there have been many times when the Phillies seldom lacked for losers. Some of them were even lovable.

The downside of Phillies history began right at the start, when, in its first year of existence, the team finished the 1883 season with a 17–81 record. Pitcher John Coleman started 65 of those games and lost an all-time record 48 of them. The Phillies yielded 20 or more runs in eight games, losing by scores as bad as 28–0 and 29–4. The team batting average was a league-worst .240.

Since then, the Phillies have finished in last place in either their division or their league 30 more times. They have finished

Fan sign acknowledging 10,000 Phillies losses, July 2007

Hugh "Losing Pitcher" Mulcahy, late 1930s

Manager James "Doc" Prothro, 1939

next to last 14 other times. And in 2007, they became the first professional sports team (with the exception of the Washington Generals, patsies of the Harlem Globetrotters) to lose 10,000 games, a calamity that attracted nationwide attention.

The Phillies also have had more no-hitters pitched against them than any other major league team. Since 1900, 17 enemy hurlers have held the Phils hitless in games that went nine or more innings. In 1960, the Phillies were no-hit by the Milwaukee Braves' Lew Burdette and Warren Spahn less than one month apart. Four other no-hitters of less than nine innings have also been inflicted on the Phils.

The dreariest era in franchise history occurred between 1918 and 1948. During that 31-year stretch, the Phils finished in the first division just once, in 1932 when they placed fourth in an eight-team league. They finished last 16 times and seventh 8 times (1 tie) during the span of futility. They lost more than 100 games in 12 different seasons, including 5 straight from 1938 to 1942.

Although it wasn't their losingest season, the low point might have been 1930, when the Phillies hit a scorching .315 as a team—the third-highest team average in National League history since 1900—but still staggered home with a record of 52–102 and a last-place finish.

Manager Eddie Sawyer, 1950s

For an explanation, one need look no further than the pitching staff, which posted an all-time team worst 6.71 earned run average. Pitchers also surrendered 1,993 hits and 1,199 runs, both major league records. "Fidgety Phil" Collins miraculously posted a 16–11 record, but six other hurlers lost in double figures, the worst being Claude "Weeping Willie" Willoughby (4–17). Three starters had ERAs over 7.50.

Poor pitching wasn't limited to 1930. Hugh Mulcahy lost 20 games in 1937 and 22 in 1940, earning him the life-long nickname, "Losing Pitcher." Five other Phillies pitchers (Eppa Rixey, George Smith, Jack Scott, Joe Bowman, and Rube Melton) lost 20 or more games in a season. In one game in 1938, hurler Hal Kelleher gave up 12 runs in one inning against the Chicago Cubs.

In 1941, under manager James "Doc" Prothro, the team dropped a club-record 111 decisions and finished 57 games behind the first-place Dodgers. It was so bad that, the following season, new manager Hans Lobert tried to change the official name of the team to the Phils, in an attempt to escape the tainted name Phillies. It didn't work. The Phils finished 42–109, 62½ games out of first. At one point, second baseman Danny Murtaugh said, "If we won a few games in a row, it might be cause for a Congressional investigation."

Another dark period in Phillies history emerged from 1958 to 1961, when the team finished last in four straight years. In

Manager Gene Mauch,
October 4, 1964

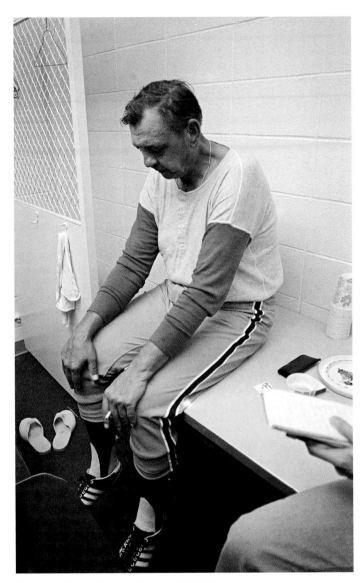

Manager Danny Ozark, October 7, 1978

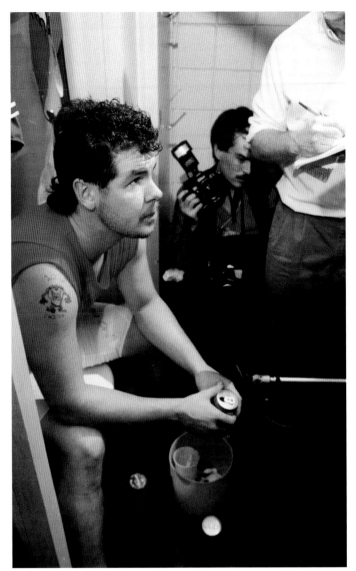

Pitcher Mitch Williams, October 23, 1993

1960, manager Eddie Sawyer quit after the first game of the season. Asked why, he said: "I'm 49, and I want to live to be 50."

In 1961, the Phillies set a record for futility by losing 23 games in a row, a mark never equaled by any other major league team. In what was Gene Mauch's first full year as manager, the club lost 107, finishing 46 games out of first place. The Phils were 17 games behind the seventh-place Cubs.

The Phillies won 92 games in 1964, the most since 1899— but it was a season in which the team earned the "loser" label perhaps more than any other. It was a good team with solid players, but it landed a place in infamy when, holding a 6½-game lead on September 20 with just 12 games left to play, it lost 10 in a row to blow the pennant. It was a collapse of such mammoth proportions that for many years thereafter it left deep scars on

the psyches of Philadelphia fans and is rivaled only by the fold of the New York Mets at the end of the 2007 season, when they lost 12 of their last 17 games.

Even though the late 1970s was the dawn of the Phillies' Golden Era, it was not without its disappointing losses. The two winningest seasons in franchise history—back-to-back records of 101–61 in 1977 and 1978—ended with exactly zero trips to the World Series.

In recent decades, the Phillies' darkest stretch was from 1987 to 2000, when they posted just 1 winning season out of 14— 1993, the year they went to the World Series. Of course, that season ended in historic fashion, as Mitch Williams gave up a series-losing home run to Toronto's Joe Carter in the final inning of Game Six.

Unusual Games

Over the years, the Phillies have played in some mighty unusual games. They've won some. They've lost some. And almost all of them defy belief.

In 1894, the Phillies beat the Louisville Colonels 29–4 while slamming an all-time record 36 hits, 6 by Sam Thompson. That year they set a record with a team batting average of .343. In 1900, the Phillies set an opening-day record with a 19–17 victory over the Boston Braves in 10 innings.

In 1922, the Phillies were victimized by the Cardinals knocking a major league record 10 consecutive hits in a 7-run inning during a 14–8 loss to St. Louis on June 12. Later that season, the Phils lost to the Chicago Cubs by a 26–23 count, a record for most runs in one game. The following year, the Phillies and Cardinals hit a combined 10 home runs in a 20–14 victory for Philadelphia.

The Phillies hit 5 home runs in the eighth inning of a 12–3 win over the Cincinnati Reds in June 1949. Andy Seminick drilled 2 of those homers, while Del Ennis, Willie Jones, and pitcher Schoolboy Rowe each hit 1 as the Phils scored 10 runs to overcome a 3–2 deficit.

On May 17, 1979, after blowing a 21–9 lead, Philadelphia defeated Chicago 23–22 in 10 innings on Mike Schmidt's home run. The New York Mets fell to the Phillies 26–7 on June 11, 1985, as the team collected 27 hits. Von Hayes hit two first-inning home runs, one a grand slam. Over the years, the Phils have also won three games by 18–0 scores and lost games by counts of 29–1 and 28–0. More recently, on July 6, 2009, they trounced Cincinnati 22–1 at home after scoring 10 runs in the first inning. Jayson Werth capped off the scoring with a ninth-inning grand slam.

Not all of the unusual Phillies feats have been achieved with a bat. One of the finest pitching performances in team history occurred in 1918 when Milt "Mule" Watson pitched a 21-inning complete game against the Cubs. Watson gave up 18 singles and a double but lost, 2–1. Another top mound job was in 1927 when Jack Scott pitched both games of a doubleheader against the Reds. He won the opener, 3–1, and lost the nightcap, 3–0. Chris Short added his name to the list of notable mound performers in 1965 when he pitched 15 shutouts innings against the Mets and struck out 18 in a scoreless game that was suspended after 18 innings.

A particularly unusual major league record was set by the Phillies in 1903 when they had nine straight home games postponed because of bad weather. In 1907, one day after heavy snow blanketed the Polo Grounds in New York, the Phils were awarded a forfeit win when fans wouldn't stop throwing snowballs. Twelve years later, the Phillies lost to the New York Giants, 6–1, in a game that was played in the unfathomable time of 51 minutes. And remember doubleheaders? The club set a record in 1943 when it played in 43 twin bills.

In 1993, the San Diego Padres beat the Phillies, 5–2, in the first game of a doubleheader. With three rain delays totaling 5 hours and 54 minutes, the game finally ended at 1 a.m. The second game started at 1:26 a.m. and wasn't decided until relief pitcher Mitch Williams, a notoriously weak hitter, singled to drive in the winning run in the 10th inning. The Phillies' 6–5 victory ended at 4:40 a.m., the latest finish for any game ever played in the majors.

Schoolboy Rowe, Del Ennis, Andy Seminick, Willie Jones, circa 1949

Left: *Jayson Werth rounding the bases after grand slam, July 6, 2009*

Below: *Mike Schmidt hitting game-winning homer, May 17, 1979*

Harry Wright, Kalamazoo tobacco card, 1887

Pat Moran, with Pat Moran Jr., 1915

THE SKIPPERS

It can never be said that Phillies managers have not been an unusual group of characters. Many of them were not especially good, but they were certainly a band of colorful individuals.

Since its origin in 1883, Philadelphia's National League ballclub has had 51 different men hold the manager's job, of which only a handful truly earned their stripes. At the summit of this group are Dallas Green and Charlie Manuel, who stand alone as the only managers to have led the Phillies to World Series victories.

Harry Wright (1884–1893), Billy Shettsline (1898–1902), Pat Moran (1915–1918), Eddie Sawyer (1948–1952, 1958–1960), Gene Mauch (1960–1968), Danny Ozark (1973–1979), Paul Owens (1972, 1983–1984), Jim Fregosi (1991–1996), and Larry Bowa (2001–2004) also all managed the Phils with distinction. Moran, Sawyer, Owens, and Fregosi each led Phillies teams to the World Series.

Several men who struggled at the helm in Philadelphia had better luck elsewhere, including six who led other teams to the Fall Classic: George Stallings (Braves), Burt Shotton (Dodgers),

Gene Mauch, 1964

Charlie Manuel, 2009

Bucky Harris (Senators), Steve O'Neil (Tigers), Mayo Smith (Tigers), and Terry Francona (Red Sox). When Shotton took the Phillies to a fourth-place finish in 1932, it marked the only time in a 31-year span (1918–1948) that the club finished in the National League's first division.

Harris, a future Hall of Famer, piloted the Phillies in 1943 but was fired during the season and later revealed that the team's president, William Cox, was betting on baseball games. Forty years later, another manager—Pat Corrales—was replaced midseason, even though the team was in first place. Ben Chapman, the Phils' manager from 1945 to 1948, was a notorious bigot who rode Jackie Robinson unmercifully during Robinson's pioneering rookie season with the Dodgers.

Many of the rest of the Phillies' managers did their best work in other endeavors. These erstwhile strategists included a practicing dentist (Doc Prothro), a vaudeville singer (Red Dooin), an alleged bigamist (Arthur Irwin), a former medical school student (Stallings), the holder of the highest single-season batting average in baseball history (Hugh Duffy, at .440), and three future umpires (Bob Ferguson, Bill Nash, and Chief Zimmer).

Overall, the Phillies have had 40 managers who had no prior managerial experience when they took the job in Philadelphia, and 31 never again managed in the big leagues after leaving the Phils. Only 16 managers had winning records with the franchise, and only 13 lasted with the team for four years or more; 14 men managed for one year or less. During the 1890 season alone, Philadelphia had four different managers because Wright came down with a case of temporary blindness. In addition to Wright, owner Al Reach, catcher Jack Clements, and rookie shortstop Bob Allen all took a turn at the reins.

Forty-two of the Phillies' pilots played in the major leagues, including 21 with the Phillies and some who had starring roles. Dooin was a catcher for 13 seasons in Philadelphia and served as player-manager for the last 5 (1910–1914). Another star backstop, Jimmie Wilson, had two stints in a playing role (1923–1928 and 1934–1938) and was also the manager during his second tenure. Outfielder Gavvy Cravath was a six-time NL home run champ for the Phils, and in 1919 and 1920 he had the job of skipper as well. Bowa was a fixture at shortstop from 1970 to 1981 before returning as manager two decades later. Two former stars of Philadelphia's *other* baseball team, the Athletics, took the managerial helm, briefly, for

the Phillies: Jack Coombs (1919) and Stuffy McInnis (1927). Five Phillies managers were natives of the Philadelphia area: Shettsline, Wilson, Hans Lobert, Green, and Lee Elia.

Bob Ferguson—with the inexplicable nickname "Death to Flying Things"—was the first Phillies pilot, and he proved to be death when it came to winning games, too. He was relieved of his duties early in the 1883 season after the team launched its maiden campaign with a 4–13 record.

The Phillies' first real manager was Wright, a skipper since leading baseball's first all-pro team, the Cincinnati Red Stockings, in 1869. Later called "The Father of Professional Baseball," Wright is credited with introducing flannel uniforms, knickers, and colored stockings to the game. He joined the Phillies in their second year, 1884, and quickly guided the team to respectability, finishing in the first division in all but the first of his 10 seasons.

Shettsline, who went from ticket-taker to manager to club president, ran the team successfully around the turn of

Danny Ozark arguing with an umpire, 1978

Dallas Green, circa 1980

the century. Then Moran led the Phillies to their first pennant in 1915; four years later he skippered the Cincinnati Reds when they met the scandalized Chicago White Sox in the 1919 World Series. Sawyer, who was a college professor during the offseason, directed the Phils to a second flag in 1950 in the first of two terms as manager

Mauch, often considered the Phillies' greatest managerial strategist, leads the franchise with most wins (646) and the most losses (684), compiled during more than eight years in Philadelphia. Ozark, a former coach with the Los Angeles Dodgers, guided the club into its most successful era, including three straight trips to the playoffs (1976–1978) and the team's all-time best single-season marks (101–61 in 1976 and 1977). He was also the source of some memorable quotes. Once, he reported that a particular player's "limitations were limitless" and that a certain situation was "beyond my apprehension." When he was relieved of his duties with 30 games to go in the 1979 season, Ozark announced that "Even Napoleon had his Watergate."

Green, an ex-Phillies pitcher and the club's former farm director, took over where Ozark left off and helped secure the team's first world championship, in 1980. He also drove the Phils to a postseason berth in the strike-split 1981 season. Two years later, Owens moved himself from the general manager's office to the dugout midway through the 1983 season in time for Philadelphia's next Fall Classic.

Fregosi, a former all-star shortstop, was the skipper for the lone bright spot of the late 1980s and 1990s when he took the Phils to the World Series in 1993. Another former all-star shortstop, the volatile Bowa, pushed the club back to a contending role during his four seasons at the helm in the early 2000s. Manuel, an ex–Japanese League star and former Cleveland Indians manager, then took the Phillies that crucial next step, with a playoff appearance in 2007 and a world championship the following year.

Manuel is the first Phillies manager to win 85 or more games in five straight seasons. He also joins Ozark as the only Phils pilots to win three division titles. Manuel—who, at 65 years of age in 2009, is the oldest man ever to manage the Phillies—ranks fourth on the club's all-time list of winningest managers, trailing only Mauch, Wright (636), and Ozark (594). He has 447 wins through the 2009 season.

Left: *Larry Bowa showing his displeasure at an umpire's call, 2001*

TEAM PRESIDENTS

Since the team began in 1883, the Phillies have been led by 15 different presidents. The group ranges from very good to absolutely awful. Some ran the team for as little as one year, while others put in many decades of service. The group has included a former manager, an ex–New York City police commissioner, a father and son, and the son of a National League president. Two Phillies presidents were banned for life from baseball for their indiscretions.

In every case, the team presidents were not sole owners of the club. Most of them represented groups of investors—and those investors changed frequently.

Among the most prominent leaders of the Phillies were the Carpenters. The Carpenter family took over the team in 1943, and 28-year-old Robert R. M. Carpenter Jr. was installed as president. Bob's father was a vice president of the hugely successful Du Pont Company, and his mother was a member of the ultra-rich duPont family. The Carpenter family was also part-owner with Connie Mack of a minor league baseball team in Wilmington, Delaware, while Bob owned a minor league basketball team there and promoted boxing matches.

The Carpenters took over a franchise that was on the verge of imploding. For decades, it had been one step away from bankruptcy. The situation was so bad that in 1942, the team was taken over by the National League and operated out of the league office by a seven-member committee.

Finally, new owners were found, and in early 1943 a 30-man syndicate led by William D. Cox, a wealthy New York lumber dealer, assumed control of the Phillies. Within less than a year, however, Cox was thrown out of organized baseball for betting on the Phillies and other teams.

The Phillies, with few talented players, no farm system, hardly any fans, and years of losing, were in shambles. But under the leadership of Bob Carpenter, the franchise was

Robert R. M. Carpenter Jr. (right) with Philadelphia Athletics owner Connie Mack, 1943

Left: *Ruly Carpenter (left) and Bill Giles, October 1981*

Below: *David Montgomery (right) with general manager Pat Gillick, 2005*

Al Reach

William Baker

turned around. Good players such as Richie Ashburn, Robin Roberts, and many others were signed, a farm system was developed, the club became solvent, and in 1950 the Phils won their first pennant in 35 years.

While that pennant was the highlight of Bob's regime, he kept the team interesting and, for much of that time, respectable, although his term was clouded by the team's failure to sign African-American players in the early years.

Bob presided over the Phillies until 1972 when his son Robert R. M. "Ruly" Carpenter III moved in. Under Ruly, the Phillies, by then well-stocked with talent, had their most successful era, winning four division titles and the World Series in 1980. They also became one of the most lucrative big-league franchises.

The Carpenters sold the club in late October 1981 to a group led by Bill Giles, a Phillies vice president whose father, Warren, had been NL president for many years. The younger Giles was the overseer of two more Phillies trips to the World

Series (1983, 1993) before stepping down as president in 1997. He would, however, remain with the team as chairman of the board and was a driving force behind building a new ballpark for the Phillies in 2004.

Current president David Montgomery began his tenure with the club in its sales department in 1971, and after moving up to vice president, he became the first Philadelphia native to head the Phils in more than six decades when he was named president in 1997. Under Montgomery, the team became one of the league's strongest franchises, built new ballparks in Philadelphia and Clearwater, and won the World Series in 2008. All the while, the team has flourished financially, regularly playing before sellout crowds.

From the Carpenters to Giles to Montgomery, the Phillies have been enormously successful. It wasn't always that way. The team's first president, Al Reach, one of baseball's earliest professional players, started the team from scratch with attorney John Rogers and made it competitive. They were forced to sell the team in 1903 when lawsuits resulting from a ballpark catastrophe and player raids by the new American League financially crippled the team.

Reach's departure was followed by a string of six short-term presidents, four of whom ran the team for two years or less. The most noteworthy of the group were Billy Shettsline, who went from ticket-taker to manager to team president, successfully guiding the team from 1905 to 1908, and Horace Fogel, former sports editor of a local newspaper who ran the Phils from 1909 to 1912. He was permanently banned from baseball for saying that the 1912 pennant race was fixed.

After two more brief presidencies, former NYC police commissioner William F. Baker bought the team in 1913. Although the Phillies won their first pennant in 1915, Baker launched the team into its worst era. A penny-pincher who regularly sold his best players, Baker presided over a period during which the team finished in sixth place or lower all but once after 1918. Baker died in office in 1930.

The Phillies remained losers after Gerald Nugent became president in 1932. Gerry had been an assistant to Baker and a highly knowledgeable baseball man. He married Mae, who was treasurer and assistant secretary of the Phils, then was named vice president and a member of the board. Ultimately, the Nugents garnered enough shares of stock in the club to take command. But the Nugents had no money themselves, constantly sold their top players, and even had to sell the office furniture at one point to help finance spring training.

During his 10 years in office, Nugent got the Phillies into the first division just once. Over one period, the team lost more than 100 games five years in a row. National League president Ford Frick finally pushed Nugent out of office in 1942, and the league operated the team until a new owner was found.

Although that was a traumatic event for the Phillies, the sorriest era in club history, one in which the team had one first division finish in 31 seasons, would soon end. Finally, for the first time since Al Reach, the team would be led by presidents who knew how to run a baseball team.

Billy Shettsline

THE DECISION-MAKERS

On a list of people who draw their paychecks from a baseball team, none is more on the hot seat than the general manager. He is the one responsible for making the trades, signing the players, hiring the manager, and performing all manner of other deeds in an attempt to build his team into a winner. If he succeeds, he's a hero. If he fails, he's a bum. With the possible exception of the manager, no one on the team goes under the microscope more than the general manager.

In a city like Philadelphia, where critics bask on every corner, general managers live in glass houses.

The Phillies have had nine general managers, but only one consistently escaped the wrath of the people. That was Paul Owens, the widely admired conductor of Phillies fortunes during the Golden Age from 1972 to 1983.

Owens' place in franchise lore was aptly assessed by former Phillies shortstop and manager Larry Bowa, who said, "Paul Owens meant more to the Phillies organization than anyone who's ever been there. He was one of a kind."

The Pope, as he was called because he bore a striking facial resemblance to Pope Paul VI, worked for the Phillies for nearly 50 years, serving as a minor league manager, scout, farm system director, general manager, manager, and ultimately a special advisor. During that time, he built the team's farm system into one of baseball's best, and as GM he guided the Phillies through its most successful era, making 46 trades along the way.

Owens drafted and signed Mike Schmidt, Greg Luzinski, Bob Boone, Bowa, and many other future Phillies standouts. He signed free agent Pete Rose and acquired Garry Maddox, Manny Trillo, Bake McBride, and Tug McGraw in trades. Under Owens

Paul Owens

Herb Pennock (second from left), with National League president Warren Giles, Cardinals president Sam Breadon, and Roy Hamey, then GM of the Pirates, 1947

Bob Carpenter (third from right) with coaching staff and other personnel, March 1950

John Quinn (left) with manager Gene Mauch and first baseman Bill White, 1966

as GM, the Phillies won their first World Series and made five postseason appearances.

Owens was an incredibly astute baseball lifer. He was also a tough, no-nonsense leader who never hesitated to jump into the middle of a fray, as he did famously in 1980 when he ripped his floundering club for its complacency. His locker room tirade helped push the Phils to the World Series.

When he saw the Phillies stumble again in 1983, he relieved himself of his GM duties and came down to the dugout (a move he had also made in 1972). Taking over near midseason, Owens managed the Phils to another World Series trip.

The first man to hold the title of general manager for the Phillies was ex-pitcher and Kennett Square, Pennsylvania, native Herb Pennock, who had the job from 1943 until he died suddenly in January 1948. Although he refused to sign African-American players, Pennock helped to build a highly productive farm system that yielded future stars such as Robin Roberts, Richie

Lee Thomas (left) with manager Jim Fregosi and team president Bill Giles, 1993 NLCS

Pat Gillick raising World Series trophy, October 2008

Ed Wade with Jim Thome, December 2002

Ruben Amaro Jr. with Raul Ibañez, December 2008

Ashburn, Curt Simmons, Granny Hamner, and Willie Jones. He also acquired a number of key veterans, including Jim Konstanty, Harry Walker, Dutch Leonard, and Johnny Wyrostek, while laying the groundwork that pushed the Phils out of the doldrums and into the World Series in 1950.

After Pennock passed away, team president Bob Carpenter served as an unofficial general manager until he hired Roy Hamey in 1954. Hamey made some good moves and some bad ones, but the Phils went downhill during his tenure.

John Quinn was named GM in 1959. Of the 51 trades made during his 14-year tenure, many were superb, including trades that brought in Johnny Callison, Tony Taylor, and Jim Bunning. Quinn also had a few clunkers, in one case swapping Dick Allen and others for a package that included Curt Flood, who refused to report to the Phillies. Quinn hired Gene Mauch as manager in 1960 and played a big role in stocking the farm system with future stars, but his biggest coup was acquiring Steve Carlton from the Cardinals in exchange for Rick Wise in 1972. It was his last deal as Phillies GM.

Owens took over for Quinn in June 1972 and held the job until 1984. Following Owens was a group called the Gang of Six that included president Bill Giles, who handled the GM duties, although not terribly effectively, until Woody Woodward was hired in October 1987. He served with no particular distinction and was relieved in June 1988.

Woodward's successor, Lee Thomas, quickly left his mark on the roster. In his first three years, Thomas made 24 trades, including ones that netted Lenny Dykstra, John Kruk, Curt Schilling, Terry Mulholland, Tommy Greene, Mitch Williams,

and a host of others who ultimately played key roles for the 1993 World Series team. The only player on the 1993 roster who was on the team when Thomas arrived in 1988 was Darren Daulton.

Thomas's assistant, Ed Wade, took over in 1997. While bringing in some major players, such as Jim Thome and Billy Wagner, Wade's term was defined, somewhat unfairly, by ill-conceived deals that sent away Schilling and Scott Rolen.

In 2005, Wade was replaced by Pat Gillick, who had spent 25 years as a highly successful GM in the American League, winning two World Series and seven division titles. With the Phillies, he made the deals and filled the holes that in 2008 produced the franchise's second World Championship.

Leading up to the championship season, Gillick traded for Brad Lidge, Joe Blanton, and Jamie Moyer and signed free agents Jayson Werth, Pedro Feliz, Greg Dobbs, Matt Stairs, and J. C. Romero. Although some of his other deals backfired (see Adam Eaton and Freddy Garcia), when he retired at the end of the 2008 season, Gillick commanded a special place among the franchise's history of GMs, second only to Paul Owens. In Gillick's four seasons with the team, the Phils won two division crowns and finished second in the other two years.

After Gillick's departure, the job went to Ruben Amaro Jr., an assistant for 10 years and a Philadelphia native who, like his father, had played with the Phillies during an eight-year big league career. Among his early acts was to sign hard-hitting free agent Raul Ibañez, and midway through the 2009 season he traded for pitcher Cliff Lee and signed free-agent pitcher Pedro Martinez, all astute moves that helped the Phillies reach the postseason and win another pennant.

TRADES

As every fan, player, and general manager knows, there is no guarantee that every trade will work out as planned. And the Phillies have ably demonstrated over the years the uncertainty of swapping players with other teams.

In late 1917, the team made two deals that exemplified both sides of the trading coin. First, on December 11, the Phils sent Grover Cleveland Alexander and catcher Bill Killefer to the Chicago Cubs for pitcher Mike Prendergast, catcher Pickles Dillhoefer, and $60,000. Alexander, only 30 years old, would go on to win 183 more games en route to Cooperstown. The 29-year-old Prendergast spent slightly more than one season with the Phillies, winning 13 games; Dillhoefer appeared in just 8 games in a Phillies uniform.

Fifteen days after that trade, the same two teams got together again, and this time the Phillies came out on the better end. Philadelphia received outfielder Cy Williams in exchange for fading 36-year-old outfielder Dode Paskert. Williams would go on to lead the National League in home runs three times; Paskert batted .257 over the next four seasons before retiring.

Bucky Walters, 1937

Ferguson Jenkins, circa 1965

As the Phillies' on-field fortunes sank to new depths in subsequent decades, their trades tended to reflect that negative trend. In 1920, they traded away two future Hall of Famers in shortstop Dave Bancroft and pitcher Eppa Rixey in separate deals and came away with almost nothing to show for it. Although his best years were behind him, Chuck Klein, another future Hall of Famer, had just completed a Triple Crown season in 1933 and earned an MVP award the year before that, when the Phils traded him to the Cubs for three bit players and cash. In similarly one-sided deals, the Phils virtually gave away pitcher Bucky Walters and first baseman Dolph Camilli in two different 1938 transactions. (Walters was the National League MVP in 1939; Camilli was NL MVP in 1941.)

Some rare bright spots in later years included acquiring Whiz Kids hero Dick Sisler in 1948, star outfielder Johnny Callison in 1959, and all-star second baseman Tony Taylor in 1960. One of the biggest acquisitions was getting Hall of Fame–bound pitcher Jim Bunning and catcher Gus Triandos for journeyman outfielder Don Demeter and pitcher Jack Hamilton after the 1963 season.

Less than three years after acquiring Bunning, however, the Phillies let another future Hall of Fame hurler go when they shipped 23-year-old Ferguson Jenkins and two utility players for over-the-hill pitchers Bob Buhl and Larry Jackson in April 1966. Although not a Hall of Famer, pitcher Jack Sanford was a former Rookie of the Year and all-star when the Phils sent him in 1958 to San Francisco for two who would never be all-stars, Ruben Gomez and Valmy Thomas.

In September 1964, hoping to add an extra bat for the stretch run, the Phillies acquired first baseman Vic Power from the Los Angeles Angels in exchange for pitcher Marcelino Lopez and a player to be named later. After the season, Power was returned to the Angels as the player to be named later.

In another odd transaction, in 1969, the Phillies sent Dick Allen and two others to the St. Louis Cardinals for four players, including Curt Flood. After refusing to report to the Phillies, Flood filed a lawsuit against Major League Baseball contesting the reserve clause, which bound players to their teams. The case went all the way to the U.S. Supreme Court, and, although Flood lost, it ultimately led to the end of the reserve clause and the start of free agency. Flood never played a game in a Phillies uniform.

Unquestionably, the Phillies' best trade of all time came in 1972 when the club sent pitcher Rick Wise to the St. Louis Cardinals for Steve Carlton. Although Wise was a fine moundsman, he was not comparable to Carlton, a future Hall of Famer and the second-winningest left-handed pitcher of all time.

Left: *Curt Flood, 1970 Topps baseball card*

Below: *Rick Wise, late 1960s*

Jamie Moyer, June 2007

Over the next few years, the Phillies came out ahead in numerous other trade acquisitions under Paul Owens' guidance, including Dave Cash (1973), Tug McGraw (1974), Garry Maddox (1975), and Manny Trillo (1979).

A decade after the blockbuster Carlton trade, Owens made one of the worst deals of his or any general manager's tenure when the Phillies traded 22-year-old second baseman and future Hall of Famer Ryne Sandberg and shortstop Larry Bowa for mediocre shortstop Ivan DeJesus.

Acquiring top-notch pitcher Curt Schilling from Houston for sub-average hurler Jason Grimsley was a savvy move by GM Lee Thomas in 1992. Ed Wade's decision in 2000 to send Schilling to Arizona was not so savvy. Wade had brought in Bobby Abreu after the 1997 season in a steal of a deal; after nine effective seasons in Philadelphia, Abreu was shipped to the Yankees with very little coming back in return.

The 2000s had more than its share of good deals and bad deals. The Phillies acquired top pitchers Billy Wagner (2003) and Jamie Moyer (2006) in trades where they got far more than they gave. More recently, sending two minor leaguers and a below-average reliever to Houston netted a vital piece for their championship drive in 2008 in ace reliever Brad Lidge, along with infielder Eric Bruntlett.

The "bad" column includes trading Gold Glove third baseman Scott Rolen to St. Louis in 2002 and, in 2006, packing off top prospect Gavin Floyd (soon to become an outstanding big league pitcher) and one other player for sore-armed hurler Freddy Garcia.

Of course, there have been many other good and bad trades. As they have often demonstrated, in the immortal words of that distinguished philosopher Mick Jagger, "You can't always get what you want."

RED-HOT ROOKIES

Since an official Rookie of the Year Award was introduced to major league baseball in 1947, as selected by the Baseball Writers' Association of America (BBWAA), four Phillies have won the prize: Jack Sanford (1957), Dick Allen (1964), Scott Rolen (1997), and Ryan Howard (2005). Others, including Del Ennis (1946), Richie Ashburn (1948), Ed Bouchee (1957), Lonnie Smith (1980), and Juan Samuel (1984), were honored as top rookies by *The Sporting News (TSN)*, which began honoring first-year players with a special award in 1946. Sanford and Ray Culp (1963) were also named Rookie Pitchers of the Year by the publication.

Although no official award was bestowed, the Phillies featured many impressive rookie performers in the first seven decades of the franchise. Ed Daily won 26 games as a pitcher for Philadelphia in 1885 while also playing 56 games in the outfield. Ben Sanders won 19 games with a 1.90 ERA and a league-best eight shutouts in 1888. In the closing year of the nineteenth century, center fielder Roy Thomas hit .325 and scored 137 runs in his first season.

Rookie George McQuillan was a 23-game winner in 1908 with a 1.53 ERA, and three years later another star hurler burst on the scene in Philadelphia. Grover Cleveland Alexander kicked off his Hall of Fame career with a 28–13 mark, 227

Buzz Arlett, 1931

Ed Daily, circa 1885

strikeouts, and a 2.57 ERA in 1911. Future Cooperstown inductee Chuck Klein got the attention of the league in his debut season of 1928 when he hit .360 in 64 games. That same season, rookie third baseman Pinky Whitney hit .301 with a team-best 103 RBI.

Buzz Arlett, a 32-year-old outfielder, made his major league debut with the Phillies in 1931. In 121 games, he hit .313 with 18 home runs and 72 RBI. After that season, Arlett never again played in the majors. His defensive skills were so bad no one wanted him.

Left fielder Ennis finished his 1946 rookie campaign with a .313 batting average, .485 slugging percentage, 17 home runs, 30 doubles, and 73 RBI—all among the league's top 10. Two years later, Ashburn joined Ennis in the Phillies outfield and hit .333,

the second-highest average in the league (behind Stan Musial), while leading the circuit in stolen bases with 32. Both Ennis and Ashburn were chosen for the all-star team in their freshman seasons, Ashburn as a starter.

In an odd turn of events in 1957, Sanford won the BBWAA award with a 19–8 record and a league-leading 188 strikeouts, while teammate first baseman Bouchee (.293–17–76) took *TSN* honors that same season. Whereas Sanford went on to establish himself as a reliable starter for more than a decade, Bouchee never again matched his rookie accomplishments and was out of baseball before he was 30. The 1957 Phillies also featured a young phenom in the bullpen: reliever Dick Farrell registered a 10–2 record with 10 saves and a 2.39 ERA in 52 games.

Jack Sanford, 1957

Ed Bouchee, 1957

Dick Allen, 1964

Dick Allen, playing third base, won the vote of both the BBWAA and *TSN* in 1964 with his .318 average, 201 hits, 29 homers, 91 RBI, and league-best 125 runs.

Playing mostly in a reserve role in left field, Lonnie Smith hit .339 and stole 33 bases in 1980 to win the *TSN* award, although he finished third in the BBWAA voting. In 1984, second baseman Samuel hit .272 with 19 homers, 69 RBI, and 105 runs while leading the league in triples (19) and at bats (701); he finished second to Dwight Gooden for the BBWAA award.

Third baseman Scott Rolen became the first Phillie in 33 years to be honored by the BBWAA when he hit .293 with 21 homers and 92 RBI in 1997. On the opposite side of the diamond, first baseman Howard played less than a full season in 2005, but his .288 average, 22 home runs, and 63 RBI in 88 games were good enough to take home the award.

Among other noteworthy rookie accomplishments, second baseman Danny Murtaugh led the league in stolen bases in 1941, and Ken Raffensberger was the winning pitcher in the 1944 All-Star Game. In more recent decades, left fielder Greg Luzinski hit .281 with 18 home runs and 68 RBI in his first full

Ryan Howard, 2005

season in 1972. Outfielder Jeff Stone broke in with a .362 batting average in 51 games in 1984. Shortstop Kevin Stocker had a superb first year in 1993, hitting .324 in 70 games after taking over shortstop duties near midseason.

The 2008 championship team featured several players who had made big splashes in their big league premieres. Shortstop Jimmy Rollins cracked the starting lineup in 2001 while leading or tying for the league lead in at bats (656), triples (12), and stolen bases (46). Second baseman Chase Utley had been up to the majors for part of two previous seasons, and he blossomed in his first full campaign in 2005, batting .291 with 28 homers and 105 RBI.

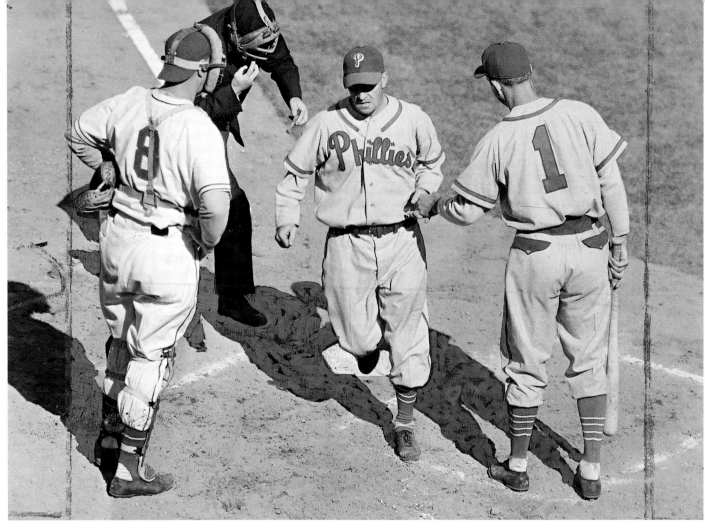

Danny Murtaugh (center), 1946

HOMEGROWN TALENT

Unfortunate as it may seem, baseball players don't always grow up to play for their hometown teams. Despite developing right under a team's nose, so to speak, local players are often the ones who got away. Sometimes teams decide against pursuing locally bred talent because they fear that playing in front of the hometown fans would put too much pressure on the player. The Phillies, however, have not always followed that philosophy. With a few exceptions—particularly in the 1950s and 1960s—the Phils have rarely shied away from signing homegrown talent. As a result, some excellent Philadelphia-area natives have grown up to wear the Phillies uniform.

Since the team began in 1883, 96 players born in the Philadelphia area (the city, four surrounding counties, South Jersey, and northern Delaware) have played for the Phillies. Forty-nine of them were natives of the city itself.

Jack Clements, a left-handed catcher from Philadelphia, hit .289 in 14 seasons with the Phils (1884–1897). One of the pitchers throwing to Clements during the late 1880s and early 1890s was Camden-born Kid Gleason. The righty hurler won 38 games in 1890 and 24 the following year before leaving for St. Louis. He returned to the Phils more than a decade later as a starting second baseman.

Philadelphia-born Bucky Walters joined the Phillies in 1934 as a third baseman before being converted to pitcher; he went on to become a three-time 20-game winner and 1939 Most Valuable Player with the Cincinnati Reds. Jimmie Wilson, the manager responsible for moving Walters to the mound, hit .288 during 11 seasons as the Phillies' catcher (1923–1928, 1934–1938), going above .300 three times.

The most successful of all the Phillies' local-born stars was Del Ennis. Rookie of the Year in 1946, a three-time

Dallas Green, early 1960s

Ruben Amaro Jr., circa 1992

National League all-star, and the league's RBI leader in 1950, he has the second-highest home run total in franchise history and ranks among the Phillies' all-time leaders in several other offensive categories. He hit 25 or more home runs in seven different seasons and exceeded 100 RBI six times.

Danny Murtaugh of Chester, Pennsylvania, was a Phillies infielder from 1941 to 1943 before being called away to military service. He rejoined the club briefly in 1946, but his greatest baseball accomplishment came decades later when he managed the cross-state rival Pittsburgh Pirates to two World Series victories.

Another future big-league skipper raised in the outskirts of the City of Brotherly Love, Dallas Green joined the Phils as a pitcher in 1960. He posted a career record of 20–22 before going on to a distinguished career as manager with the Phillies, Yankees, and Mets and front-office leader with the Chicago Cubs.

Ruben Amaro Jr. was born in Philadelphia in 1965 when his father, Ruben Amaro Sr., was an infielder for the Phillies. The younger Amaro played in the Phils' outfield (1992–1993, 1996–1998) before becoming the team's general manager in 2008.

Pitcher Jamie Moyer, born in Sellersville in Bucks County and a graduate of Saint Joseph's University in Philadelphia, joined his hometown team in his 20th major league season, in 2006.

Among the other notable Philadelphia-area natives who spent time with the Phillies were outfielder Roy Thomas (1899–1908, 1910–1911); infielders Monte Cross (1898–1901), Hans Lobert (1911–1914), and Rick Schu (1984–1987, 1991); catcher Mike Grady (1894–1897); and pitchers Lefty Weinert (1919–1924), Johnny Podgajny (1940–1943), Frank Hoerst (1940–1942, 1946–1947), Jack Meyer (1955–1961), Bobby Shantz (1964), and Rawly Eastwick (1978–1979).

CATCHERS

The men behind the plate. Backstops. Receivers. Catchers. Regardless of what they're called, those charged with the duty of snaring pitches and handling all kinds of other vital tasks are widely considered the most important position players on the field.

In this department, the Phillies have not been short-changed. Although there are no Hall of Famers among them, numerous catchers have shown substantial merit with the Phils, many of them with more than one claim to fame.

Jack Clements was left-handed. Red Dooin and Jimmie Wilson both became Phils managers. Bill Atwood flew airplanes with Eddie Rickenbacher. Bob Boone's father and two sons played in the major leagues. Ozzie Virgil's father did, too. And Darren Daulton was one of the most popular players in team history.

The top hitter on the inaugural 1883 Phillies team was catcher Emil Gross (.307), who shared backstop duties with the poor-hitting but more-reliable-fielding Frank Ringo. Philadelphia had no fewer than a dozen men take a turn behind the plate in 1884, until Clements emerged as a steady presence beginning in 1885.

One of the first catchers to wear a chest protector, Clements played 14 seasons for the Phillies (1884–1897) and caught more games than any left-handed receiver in baseball history. He finished among the league's top four hitters three times, with a high of .394 in 1895, and four other times hit above .300. He also had decent power for the era, ranking among the top 10 home run hitters five times between 1890 and 1897.

Jack Clements, 1887

Red Dooin, 1913

Jimmie Wilson, 1936

Andy Seminick, 1951

Ed McFarland was acquired from St. Louis in June 1897, and he caught ably for the Phillies through 1901. He caught in 121 games in 1898 and batted over .300 in each of the next two seasons before jumping to the American League in 1902. Red Dooin, a mediocre hitter but a solid defensive catcher, stepped in and remained with the club until 1914, the last five seasons as player-manager. Dooin was one of the first backstops to wear shin guards.

Another good-field, mostly no-hit catcher assumed the duties from 1912 to 1917. Bill Killefer's biggest contribution was helping to turn the raw Grover Cleveland Alexander into a Hall of Famer.

Butch Henline, who had played in one major league game before coming to the Phils as part of an atrocious trade that sent outfielder Irish Meusel to the New York Giants, proved to be a pleasant surprise, hitting .304 during his six years in Philadelphia (1921–1926). Then came Wilson, a native Philadelphian who put in two terms (1923–1928, 1934–1938) with the team, the second as a player-manager. A fine hitter who hit .328 in 1925, Wilson once made 18 putouts in a game and another time had no fielding chances in a 13-inning contest.

Walt "Peck" Lerian was the Phillies' main backstop in 1928 and 1929. Shortly after his second season, he was killed while standing on a Baltimore street corner when a vehicle,

Bob Boone, late 1970s

Darren Daulton, 1995

trying to avoid another vehicle, jumped the curb and pinned him against a building. That tragedy moved Spud Davis into the starting lineup. Davis, who had been acquired from the Cardinals in a May 1928 trade for Wilson, excelled on offense and defense. He committed only three errors during the 1931 season to set a franchise record for catchers with a .994 fielding percentage. He batted over .300 every year from 1929 to 1933, including a high of .349 in 1933, second only to teammate Chuck Klein in the batting race. The following offseason, Davis was traded back to St. Louis, again in exchange for Jimmie Wilson. Davis returned to Philadelphia in June 1938 and spent another season and a half with the Phillies.

A string of different catchers took a turn in the early 1940s, including Bill Atwood, later a decorated World War II and commercial pilot. Andy Seminick became the regular

receiver in 1945. An astute handler of pitchers and a leader on the field, Seminick was a power hitter who twice hit 24 home runs in a season. He had two terms (1943–1951, 1955–1957) with the Phils.

In between Seminick's two stints, Smoky Burgess was the primary catcher. He hit .368 in an all-star 1954 season. Stan Lopata first joined the Phillies in 1948, and he finally got his shot at regular action in 1955. He responded by making the all-star team that year, a feat he repeated in 1956 when he hit 32 homers, scored 96 runs, and drove in 95.

Clay Dalrymple, an average hitter but a defensive standout, caught for the Phillies from 1960 to 1968. Dalrymple was followed by the likes of Mike Ryan (a career .193 hitter) and Tim McCarver, until the emergence of Bob Boone. Converted from third base to catcher by Seminick, one of his managers in the minors, Boone became the

Mike Lieberthal, 2000

Carlos Ruiz, 2009

starting backstop for the big league club in 1973, a job he held through 1981. The Stanford University grad was a team leader and one of the smartest men on the field. A Gold Glove Award winner in 1978 and 1979 and no slouch as a hitter—he averaged .282 from 1976 to 1979—Boone was a key player on the 1980 World Series team. A strong case could be made that Boone was the best catcher in modern Phillies history.

Bo Diaz and Ozzie Virgil followed Boone, and in 1987 the Phillies picked up free-agent Lance Parrish, but the former Detroit Tigers all-star proved to be a huge disappointment in two seasons with Philadelphia. Ultimately, he was replaced by Daulton, who after first appearing in Philly in 1983, became the regular catcher from 1989 through 1995. A team leader who ruled from a reclining chair in front of his locker, Daulton became only the fourth National League catcher

to lead the league in RBI (109) in 1992. One year later, he led the league again with 105. Injuries gradually slowed his career, and in 1997 he played exclusively at first base and in the outfield before being traded in midseason to Florida, where he won a World Series ring.

The last of the long-term catchers was Mike Lieberthal, the third overall pick in the 1990 draft. After backing up Daulton, he became the starter for nine years beginning in 1997. Lieberthal had the best all-around season of any Phillies catcher in 1999, when he hit .300 with 31 home runs and 96 RBI. He also won a Gold Glove that year. A two-time all-star, Lieberthal caught more games (1,139) than any other Phils catcher.

Carlos Ruiz, who succeeded Lieberthal in 2007, promises to join this group of excellent Phillies catchers. He batted .375 during the World Series win over Tampa Bay in 2008.

Sid Farrar, 1887

Fred Luderus, circa 1917

FIRST BASEMEN

There is nothing nebulous about the requirements of a first baseman. Quite clearly, a first baseman must be a good hitter, preferably one who can hit with power. If he can field adequately, so much the better.

Most teams go out of their way to ensure that their lineups have first basemen who fit these specifications. The Phillies have been no exception, and the club has a long line of first sackers who satisfy the requirements of the position.

No one has done that better than the team's current first baseman. In his first five years, Ryan Howard has already established himself among the Phillies' all-time home run leaders. And he is quickly advancing on the all-time home run leaders among all major league first basemen.

Howard unquestionably ranks at the top of the franchise list of first basemen, but he's certainly not the only star Phillie at the position. Sid Farrar was the team's first first baseman in 1883, and he played more than 800 games there through 1890—although

his biggest claim to fame may be his daughter, Geraldine, who was a world-famous opera singer in the opening decades of the twentieth century. Sid Farrar, a mere .253 career hitter, did sing in his church choir.

After Farrar, the next first baseman of note was Jack Boyle (1893–1895), the Phillies' first captain. A decade later, Kitty Bransfield (1905–1910) held the spot, hitting as high as .304 in 1908. In between, a series of Hall of Famers manned the position for brief periods, including Roger Connor (1892), Dan Brouthers (1896), Nap Lajoie (1897), Ed Delahanty (1900), and Hughie Jennings (1901–1902).

Fred Luderus took over in 1911, and before stepping down as a regular in 1919, he played in more games (1,298) than any other Phils first baseman. Luderus, who became team captain, was one of the stars of the 1915 pennant-winning squad. He hit .315 during the regular season, second highest in the league, and .438 in the World Series. A weak fielder who once committed 30

Dolph Camilli, 1937

Eddie Waitkus, 1950

errors in a season, Luderus finished second in the league in home runs in 1911 and 1913. At one point he played in a then-record 533 straight games.

A string of first basemen followed, including Walt Holke, who hit .311 and .300 in 1923 and 1924, respectively, and Nelson "Chicken" Hawks, who batted .322 in his lone season in 1925. Don Hurst became the regular in 1928 and, in his six years, hit above .300 four times while averaging 22 home runs, including 31 in 1929. In 1932, he hit .339 with 24 homers and a league-high 143 RBI. In June 1934, he was traded to the Chicago Cubs for Dolph Camilli, another hard-hitting first baseman. Camilli went .315–28–106 in 1936 and .339–27–101 the following year. The Phillies traded Camilli to the Brooklyn Dodgers in 1938, and three years later, he was named the NL's Most Valuable Player.

Another parade of first basemen passed through Philadelphia in the 1940s, including Nick Etten (1941–1942), who in 1944 led the American League in home runs as a Yankee; Babe Dahlgren, an all-star reserve during his one season in Philadelphia (1943); Hall of Famer Jimmie Foxx (1945); Frank McCormick, who hit .284 and made just one error in 135 games during his 1946 all-star

campaign; and Dick Sisler, later the hero of the 1950 season as an outfielder. Eddie Waitkus came over from the Cubs in 1949, but in midseason he was shot in a hotel room by a deranged woman during a Phillies road trip to Chicago. Miraculously, Waitkus survived and came back to play in 1950, hitting .284 for the pennant-winning Phils. One of the top-fielding first basemen in team history, Waitkus was a regular until 1953.

Ed Bouchee appeared to be the first baseman of the future after winning Rookie of the Year honors in 1957 with a .293 average, 17 homers, and a team-high 76 RBI, but he only lasted through 1959. From 1960 to 1978, Juan "Pancho" Herrera, Roy Sievers, Dick Stuart, Bill White, Dick Allen, Deron Johnson, Willie Montanez, and Richie Hebner all took turns at first. In 1964 alone, the Phils used nine different players at the initial sack. While Stuart earned the nicknames "Stonehands" and "Dr. Strangeglove" for his famously atrocious fielding, White in 1966 became the only first baseman in franchise history to win a Gold Glove Award. Stuart once asserted that "errors are part of my image," and on one occasion he went to the mound after a pickoff throw by Jim Bunning and urged the Phils hurler not to throw so hard.

Pete Rose, 1980 World Series

John Kruk, 1993

Pete Rose was signed as a free agent in 1979, hit .331, and restored some stability to the position. "Charlie Hustle" helped spark the Phillies to victory in the 1980 World Series and again to the pennant in 1983. He appeared in four straight All-Star Games as a Phillie (1979–1982).

In 1986, Von Hayes shifted from the outfield to first and stayed there for three seasons. He had a career year in 1986, with a .305 average, 19 homers, and 98 RBI along with league highs in runs scored (107) and doubles (46). Hayes returned to the outer pastures with the arrival of John Kruk from San Diego in June 1989. Kruk was selected to three all-star teams and batted .309 as a Phillie from 1989 to 1994. His .316 average was tops among the full-season regulars on the 1993 pennant-winning squad. Kruk also batted .348 in the Fall Classic.

Rico Brogna was an exquisite fielder who averaged 21 homers and 96 RBI in three full seasons (1997–1999) as the Phillies first sacker. All-star Jim Thome signed as a free agent in 2003 and led the league with 47 homers while driving in 131 runs. He hit 42 homers in 2004, but by 2005 it was time to make room for Ryan Howard.

The young slugger led the league in home runs and RBI in 2006 and again in 2008. In his first full major league season (2006), Howard established a new club record for homers (58) in one season; only nine other times in big league history has a player hit more four-baggers in a single season. The powerful first baseman was also the National League's Rookie of the Year in 2005 and its Most Valuable Player in 2006 (and runner-up in 2008).

In addition to the impressive on-field accomplishments, some Philadelphia first basemen had other noteworthy resume items, too. Gene Paulette (1920) was banned for life from baseball for allegedly taking money from gamblers. Art Mahan (1940) became the long-time baseball coach and athletic director at Philadelphia's Villanova University. Dahlgren was Lou Gehrig's replacement when the "Iron Horse" stepped down in 1939. Howie Schultz (1947) was a former pro basketball player. Bill White (1966–1968) became president of the National League. Richie Hebner (1977–1978) had an offseason job digging graves.

Ryan Howard, 2008

SECOND BASEMEN

Often overshadowed but seldom overrated, second basemen play a valuable role in the fabric of any baseball team. Good second basemen need to be able to go to their right and go to their left in the field. They need to go back; they need to come in. They need to be able to turn double plays. And they need strong arms for relays. It helps, of course, if they can hit, too.

Although, for the most part, the Phillies' legacy of second basemen is not overwhelming, the position does have an interesting history in franchise annals, starting with Bob Ferguson, the team's very first second baseman. Ferguson was the club's manager in 1883 but was fired from that role after 17 games. He went back to his old position at the keystone sack and hit an uninspiring .258. He also made 88 errors in 85 games, which ties an all-time major league record.

As the Phillies improved their place in the standings after the Ferguson fiasco, their talent at second base gradually improved as well. Bill Hallman took a firm hold on the position in 1892, and over the next five seasons, he hit above .300 four times, including a high of .320 in 1896. He was traded to St. Louis in 1897, and the following season the 22-year-old Napoleon Lajoie shifted from first base to the keystone

Bill Hallman, 1888

Emil Verban, 1947

position. The future Hall of Famer batted .324 and led the league with 43 doubles and 127 RBI that year. He hit .378 in 1899 and .337 in 1900 before jumping to the Athletics of the upstart American League, where he batted .426 and won the Triple Crown.

Hallman, meanwhile, jumped back to the Phillies from Cleveland's AL club in 1901 and reclaimed his job at second. Two years later, another former Phillies star returned home after an 11-year hiatus. A 38-game winner as a pitcher for the Phils in 1890, Kid Gleason eventually threw out his arm and became an infielder for other teams. In 1903, he was traded to Philadelphia, where he manned second base for four years.

Tony Taylor, circa 1964

Otto "Dutch" Knabe succeeded Gleason from 1907 through 1913, and for a long time afterward, the Phillies fielded a flock of mediocre second sackers, until Fresco Thompson came over from the New York Giants in a 1927 trade. Thompson played the post with distinction for the next four seasons, hitting as high as .324 in 1929. The position then went dormant again as the Phils fielded a different second baseman nearly every year until Danny Murtaugh grabbed the spot for three seasons in the early 1940s.

Emil Verban, a superb fielder and decent hitter, spent two and a half seasons with Philadelphia and played in the 1946 and 1947 All-Star Games before being waived in midseason 1948. Granny Hamner slid over from shortstop to fill in for the remainder of 1948 and, after switching back to short, returned to second for a few more seasons in the 1950s. He was the National League's starting second baseman in the 1954 All-Star Game.

The acquisition of Tony Taylor from the Chicago Cubs in 1960 gave the Phillies another all-star pivot man. Taylor spent six strong seasons at the position before moving to third base later in the decade. In all, he played 1,003 games at second base for the Phillies, more than anyone else in franchise history.

Cookie Rojas was an all-around utility man before settling in at second during the 1965 season, where he remained as the starter for the next four years. After the 1969 season, Rojas was sent to St. Louis as part of the ill-fated Curt Flood deal.

The Phillies acquired Dave Cash from the Pittsburgh Pirates for pitcher Ken Brett in 1974, just as the club was launching its greatest era. Firing up his teammates with the slogan, "Yes, We Can," Cash was a standout performer and team leader for the next three years, twice hitting .300 and leading the league with 213 hits in 1975. He was an all-star in all three seasons with Philadelphia.

Ted Sizemore was the second baseman for the division champs in 1977 and 1978. Before the 1979 season, Sizemore was part of an eight-player deal with the Cubs that brought Manny Trillo to Philadelphia. Over the next four seasons, Trillo stamped his name as the club's all-time best fielding second sacker. The three-time Gold Glove winner and two-time Silver Slugger also posted a .381 batting average in the 1980 National League Championship Series against the Houston Astros and made a crucial relay throw to cut down a run at the plate in the fifth game. He was named the NLCS Most Valuable Player.

Hall of Famer Joe Morgan took a one-year turn for the Phillies in 1983 before homegrown product Juan Samuel burst on the scene in 1984. A strong offensive force in the lineup, Samuel became the first major leaguer to reach double figures in doubles, triples, home runs, and stolen bases in each of his first four seasons. Although he struck out a league-worst 168 times in his debut year, Samuel's speed produced 72 stolen bases—more than any Phillies player since 1895—105 runs, and 19 triples, which tied for the league lead, en route to an all-star selection (although he did not enter the game). He earned another trip to the midseason classic in 1987, when he notched career highs in homers (28), RBI (100), and runs (113) while batting .272.

After two seasons with veteran Tom Herr at second base, in 1991 the Phillies gave the job to another homegrown talent in Mickey Morandini, who provided stability at the position for seven seasons. In 1992, he became the first second baseman to register an unassisted triple play during the regular season. An excellent defensive player, Morandini was also a solid hitter, twice hitting over .290. Mariano Duncan shared second-base duties with Morandini from 1992 to 1994 and was voted as the NL's All-Star Game starter at the position in

Manny Trillo, 1980 World Series

Juan Samuel, 1986

1994—even though Morandini ended up playing twice as many games at second as Duncan did.

While Marlon Anderson and Placido Polanco adequately manned the pivot after Morandini, the Phillies' next second baseman quickly established himself as the franchise's all-time best at the position. Chase Utley, a first-round pick in 2000, became the regular starter in 2005. In his first five full seasons (2005–2009), he has hit more than 30 homers three times, driven in 100 or more runs four times, and batted above .300 twice, including the league's third-highest average (.332) in 2007. He won the Silver Slugger Award for second basemen in three straight seasons while also earning four straight All-Star Game appearances.

In addition to Gleason, who managed the infamous Chicago Black Sox in 1919, and Murtaugh, who skippered the Pirates to two World Series championships, the roster of former Phillies second basemen also includes Sparky Anderson, who played the position in 1959 and decades later went on to become a three-time World Series winner as manager with the Cincinnati Reds and Detroit Tigers. Fresco Thompson was a key front-office figure for the Brooklyn Dodgers in the 1950s.

Mickey Morandini, 1997

Chase Utley, 2008 World Series

THIRD BASEMEN

The best player in Philadelphia Phillies history was a third baseman. Beyond that, however, the hot corner has been largely a lean position for the franchise, and at times third basemen came and went about as often as the city held its annual Mummer's Day Parade.

That is not to say that no other third sackers deserve mention. Joe Mulvey was a guardian of the hot corner from 1884 to 1889, one of only a handful of Phillies third baseman who stuck around the starting lineup for more than four years. In his debut season with Philadelphia, Mulvey hit .229 and made 73 errors during the year, including 6 in one game. The following season, he increased his average by 40 points and cut the number of errors to 62. By 1889, Mulvey posted a career-high .289 batting average but still managed to flub 54 plays in the field.

Third baseman Lave Cross batted .386 for the 1894 club—which was only good enough for fifth-best on a roster that featured four .400 hitters. Philadelphia didn't have another third baseman reach the .300 mark until "Fighting" Harry Wolverton hit .309 in 1901.

The starting third baseman from 1908 to 1910 was a career .249 hitter, but Eddie Grant earned a place in baseball chronicles as the first major league baseball player killed in World War I. Hans Lobert followed Grant in Philadelphia, playing the hot corner respectably from 1911 to 1914, twice stealing 40 or more bases and batting .293 over the four-year stretch.

Milt Stock played third for the Phillies from 1916 to 1918, and he was Bobby Byrne's backup on the team's first pennant winner, in 1915. Thirty-five years later, when the Phils won their next pennant in 1950, Stock was the Brooklyn Dodgers' third-base

Joe Mulvey, 1887

Milt Stock, 1915

coach who sent Cal Abrams home in the bottom of the ninth inning of the last game of the season. Instead of scoring the winning run, Abrams was thrown out easily by Richie Ashburn, and the Phillies went on to win an inning later.

After Stock, only Russ Wrightstone held down the position for more than two seasons (1921, 1923–1924) until Pinky Whitney came along in 1928. Playing for terrible Phillies teams from 1928 to 1932 and again (after a three-year interlude with the Boston Braves) from 1936 to 1938, Whitney batted over .300 during his tenure in Philadelphia, posting a .342 mark in 1930 and .341 in 1937. A fine fielder, he also drove in more than 100 runs in four of his first five seasons, with a high of 124 in 1932. Only Mike Schmidt and Willie Jones played more games at third for the Phillies.

Whitney was followed by another Pinky, Merrill "Pinky" May, in 1939. A .275 career hitter, May spent five seasons as a starter and thrice led the league in fielding. Between 1943 and 1949, the Phillies had a different third baseman each year until Jones established himself as a long-term solution. Jones first appeared in 18 games in 1947 and 17 more in 1948, but he averaged 146 games played over the next nine seasons. Nicknamed "Puddin' Head,"

Jones hit home runs in double figures nine times, including a high of 25 for the pennant-winning Whiz Kids in 1950. He also led the league in fielding five times and shares the record for most years leading the league in putouts (seven).

After Jones was traded to Cleveland in June 1959, the Phillies had another revolving door installed at third base, with five different starters in five seasons. Although that crew included *former* all-stars Alvin Dark (1960) and Don Hoak (1963), it wasn't until the arrival of Dick Allen that the team had a *current* all-star at the position.

Allen took over the hot corner in 1964 and became one of the club's greatest hitters while playing there through 1967 (after which he switched to first base). He earned Rookie of the Year honors in 1964 for his .318 average, 29 homers, and league-leading 125 runs scored. Allen staged his best performance in 1966, batting .317 with 40 home runs and 110 RBI. He was a weak fielder but had excellent speed, posting double digits in triples every year from 1964 to 1967 and stealing a team-high 20 bases in 1967. One of the team's few bright spots of the 1960s, Allen's career in Philadelphia was

Pinky Whitney, circa 1928

Willie Jones, 1950

marked by controversy, and in 1969 the team felt it necessary to trade him. Allen returned to the Phils in 1975 and stayed for two seasons, playing first base.

Tony Taylor, shifted over from second base, and Don Money handled most of the work at the hot corner through 1973, when along came Michael Jack Schmidt. The best player in franchise history got off to a rocky start, batting .196 and striking out 136 times in 367 at bats during his rookie season. A year later, while playing in all 162 games, the future Hall of Famer arrived. His average jumped to .282, and he led the National League in home runs (36) and slugging average (.546)—as well as strikeouts (138)—while finishing second in runs scored (108) and runs batted in (116). He earned his first all-star selection.

Not only is Schmidt regarded as the best player in team history, a good case can be made that he's the best third baseman baseball has ever had. His credentials certainly back that up: three-time Most Valuable Player (1980, 1981, 1986); 14th all-time in career home runs (548); 12-time all-star; 10-time Gold Glove winner; six-time Silver Slugger; and first-ballot inductee

Dick Allen, 1964

Mike Schmidt, 1980 World Series

to the Baseball Hall of Fame. And that's only a few of the noteworthy achievements in Schmidt's extraordinary career.

Schmidt, who heads the franchise's all-time list in most major hitting categories, was a five-tool player who, from his major league debut in 1972 to his retirement in 1989—a span that gave him more years with the Phils than any other player—was the mainstay in the most successful era in club history, a period that included two World Series teams and six trips to postseason playoffs.

Following the retirement of the Phillies icon, Charlie Hayes (1989–1991, 1995) and Dave Hollins (1992–1994) filled in admirably until Scott Rolen took over in 1997 and won Rookie of the Year honors after hitting .283 with 21 home runs and 92 RBI. An exceptional fielder who won three Gold Gloves as a member of the Phillies, Rolen hit in double figures in home runs in all six years with the team, reaching a high of 31 in 1998. Rolen's time with the Phillies was marred by injuries and mediocre teams. Eventually, his relationship with the team soured, and he became the target of the boo-birds before getting traded to the Cardinals in a deadline deal in 2002.

Pedro Feliz, a free-agent signing before the 2008 season, was at the hot corner for the championship team that year. An outstanding defensive player, in 2009 he posted one of the best offensive seasons of his 10-year career.

Scott Rolen, 1998

Pedro Feliz, 2009

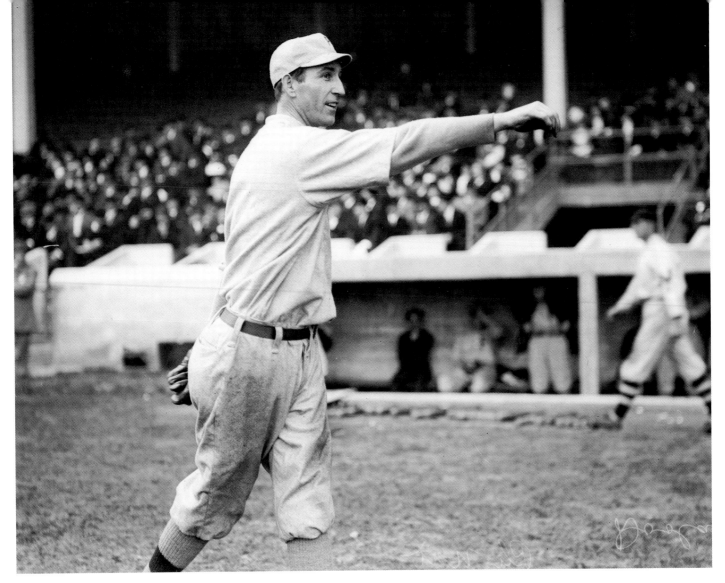

Mickey Doolan, 1912

SHORTSTOPS

Good shortstops are, first and foremost, good fielders. A good shortstop can't be laid back. A good shortstop is aggressive, always on the move, hustling as he goes. Often, his uniform is dirty by the fourth inning.

Shortstop is the most demanding position of all the fielders. Generally, more balls are hit to shortstops than to any other fielder. They are hit in any number of different ways and speeds, and it is the shortstop's job to stop them all. And then he has to throw with deadly accuracy and, if necessary, make double plays.

Not always, but sometimes, shortstops who are good on defense are good hitters, too. The Phillies have had some shortstops who fall into this good-field, good-hit category. Five, in particular, stand out above the rest.

Dave Bancroft, Dick Bartell, Granny Hamner, Larry Bowa, and Jimmy Rollins were outstanding in all phases of the game. Bancroft is in the Hall of Fame. Bartell was the National League's starting shortstop in the first All-Star Game in 1933. Hamner was the sparkplug and captain of the 1950 Whiz Kids. Bowa holds the highest career fielding percentage (.980) for a shortstop in National League history. Rollins was the NL Most Valuable Player in 2007. And all except Bartell anchored the infields of Phillies pennant-winners. Bancroft, Bartell, and Bowa all finished their careers with more than 2,000 hits and Rollins is well on his way.

Dave Bancroft, 1915

Dick Bartell, 1932

After the Phillies began, it took a while to get a decent shortstop. Their first one in 1883 was Bill McClellan. He lasted just two years after making 159 errors in that time.

A legion of mid-fielders followed, none the least bit distinguished. There were, however, two with special designations. One was Bob Allen, who as a rookie in 1890 was one of four men who managed the Phillies that year. He was called to the job when regular manager Harry Wright suffered a temporary loss of sight and had to take a break. The other shortstop of note during the early years was Billy Hulen, who had the rare trait of being left handed. No other team ever had a regular left-handed shortstop.

Mickey Doolan was the first Phillies shortstop of any real stature, holding the job from 1905 to 1913. A .230 career hitter, he was rated as one of the top defensive shortstops in the league and was the first Phil at that position to lead the league in

fielding (1910). He ranks third on the franchise list of most games played (1,297) at shortstop.

Bancroft arrived in 1915 and as a rookie was a major cog in the Phillies' first pennant. Banny posted mediocre numbers during his more than five seasons as a Phils regular, but he was blossoming and hitting .298 in 1920 when the team sent him to the New York Giants in one of many ill-advised trades made by owner William Baker. Bancroft went on to become the premier shortstop in the NL, hitting over .300 five times. He was elected into the Hall of Fame in 1971.

The team lacked a premier shortstop during the 1920s, although Heinie Sand (1923–1928) won acclaim for reporting a gambler who tried to bribe him to throw a game in 1924. Sand also led the league in fielding that year.

Bartell, one of the scrappiest players in baseball, spent four years (1931–1934) with the team and became the Phils' captain.

Granny Hamner, circa 1950

Bobby Wine, 1962

While ranking among the top defensive shortstops, he twice hit over .300 and was one of the game's best bunters. In a game in 1933, Bartell became the first major leaguer to hit four consecutive doubles.

After Bartell, the Phils had 11 different men take a turn as the regular shortstop over the next 14 years. Bobby Bragan had the longest stay: three seasons (1940–1942).

Hamner broke in with the Phils in 1944 at the age of 17. A fiery battler, he took over the starting shortstop job in 1948, and although he covered second base for a few years, he stayed with the club through 1959. A clutch hitter and excellent fielder, Hamner was one of the Whiz Kids' most popular players.

The Phillies again struggled to find a reliable presence at mid-field after Hamner. Bobby Wine, a Gold Glove winner in 1963, covered the position from 1962 to 1967, sharing time with Ruben Amaro Sr. Amaro won the Gold Glove Award for shortstop in 1964, a year after Wine. Amaro is also father of the team's current general manager.

Bowa was without peer as a defensive shortstop, and during his lengthy career in Philadelphia (1970–1981), he led the league in fielding five times, in 1979 posting a then-record .991 average. In 1972, he made just nine errors the entire season. A two-time Gold Glove winner, Bowa was named to five all-star teams. Another cocky, feisty scrapper, the switch-hitting future Phillies manager was a solid batsman who hit .305 in 1975. Bowa played in more games (1,730) than any other Phils shortstop.

In January 1982, Bowa was traded, along with a young infield prospect named Ryne Sandberg, to the Cubs for Ivan DeJesus. DeJesus filled the gap at short from 1982 to 1984, followed by Steve Jeltz (1985–1988) and Dickie Thon (1989–1991). Kevin Stocker was called up in midseason of 1993 and batted .324 in 70 games for the pennant winners. Stocker remained with the team through 1997.

The next truly great Phillies shortstop was Jimmy Rollins, who joined the team in 2001. Since then, he has won two Gold Gloves, made three all-star teams, and won a Silver Slugger Award. Through his first eight years as a starter, Rollins had already hit more home runs (125) than any other Phils shortstop. He trails only Bowa in most games played at the position. Owner of the longest hitting streak in team history (38 games), Rollins had his biggest year in 2007 when he batted .296 with 30 home runs and 94 RBI while leading the league in at bats (715), runs (139), and triples (20) to win the MVP trophy.

Larry Bowa, 1980 World Series

Jimmy Rollins, 2009

OUTFIELDERS

If there's one area of the Phillies lineup than has consistently been filled by exceptional players, it's the outfield. Almost from the start, the team has been staffed by outfielders who are among the game's best.

In addition to boasting six Hall of Famers, Phillies outfielders have won 16 home run titles, captured 9 batting crowns, and led the National League in RBI 14 times. They've been named to all-star teams 25 times and won 11 Gold Gloves. And there is a two-time Most Valuable Player among them.

The parade of Phillies outfielders began somewhat unusually when, in 1883, left fielder Blondie Purcell became the team's manager 17 games into the season. Purcell was removed as skipper at the end of the campaign, returning to the outfield. There he rejoined a group of mediocre fly-catchers who dominated the roster until Sam Thompson arrived in 1889 and became the Phillies' first home run champ.

Two years later, Billy Hamilton won Philadelphia's first batting title as part of an outfield that also included Thompson and Ed Delahanty. Playing together until 1895, the threesome became the only outfield in baseball history who would all earn entry into the Hall of Fame. In 1894, they became the only outfield trio to all bat over .400 in the same season. Delahanty ranks first on the Phillies career list in doubles and triples and second in RBI, runs,

singles, extra base hits, and total bases. He hit .348 as a Phillie, which is second to Hamilton's .361 on the all-time franchise roster. Thompson hit .333 in his 10 seasons as a Phillie, although he captured two home run crowns during that time.

Hamilton, who won two batting titles with the Phillies, was traded to Boston after the 1895 season, and the following June Philadelphia acquired Duff Cooley from St. Louis to fill his place. Cooley had three straight years batting over .300 (1896–1898). Elmer Flick joined Cooley as a 22-year-old rookie in 1898 and went on to post four straight seasons over .300, including .367 in 1900 while driving in a league-leading 110 runs (one more than teammate Delahanty). Two years later, Flick jumped to the new American League. By then, Roy Thomas had become a key member of the Phillies outfield, and after setting a rookie record with 137 runs scored in 1899, he hit above .300 in five of his first seven seasons in the league. He also led the league in walks seven times in an eight-year period.

John Titus (1903–1912) and Sherry Magee (1904–1914) both came along early in the twentieth century. Titus was a solid .280 hitter, while Magee won a batting title in 1910 and hit over .300 in 5 of his 11 seasons with the Phillies. In 1910, he also led the NL in runs, RBI, and slugging percentage. Magee is third on the Phillies' all-time list for stolen bases (387) and second in triples (127). He

Gavvy Cravath, Dode Paskert, and Possum Whitted, 1915

Dick Sisler, Richie Ashburn, and Del Ennis, 1951

was also once suspended for KO'ing an umpire during a heated discussion after a called third strike. Eight years later, Magee became an umpire himself.

Gavvy Cravath arrived in 1912, 31 years old and with limited big league experience, and proceeded to win six home run titles in seven years. In 1913, he led the league in both homers and RBI and finished second in batting average, with a career-best .341 mark. Two years later, he again led in homers and RBI, as well as runs, walks, and slugging percentage. Cravath was the premier home run hitter in the business until his records were broken by Babe Ruth.

Dode Paskert (1911–1917) played alongside Cravath for six seasons and posted a career-high .315 average in 1912. At the end of the 1917 season, Paskert was traded for another top outfielder, Cy Williams. Emil "Irish" Meusel joined the team in 1918 but was shipped to the Giants in July 1921 while he was hitting .353. Williams remained with the club for 13 seasons and was one of the few bright spots during the Phillies' woeful years of the 1920s. He hit above .300 six times in seven seasons and won three home run crowns while in Philadelphia. His 41 dingers in 1923 make him one of only six Phillies in history to hit at least 40 homers in one season.

Raul Ibañez, Shane Victorino, and Jayson Werth, 2009

Fred Leach was a .312 hitter with the Phillies (1923–1928) before being traded for Lefty O'Doul. The trade brought immediate dividends. O'Doul led the league in 1929 with a .398 average while collecting 254 hits in 1929, which still stands as the single-season National League record (shared with Bill Terry of the Giants). O'Doul followed with a .383 season in 1930 and then was traded to the Dodgers.

Meanwhile, Chuck Klein broke in with the Phils in 1928 and, by the time he retired in 1944, had three separate stints with the team and was setting up a trip to Cooperstown. He led the league in home runs four times and RBI twice, had five consecutive seasons with 200 or more hits, and batted .359 over his first six years in the league. In 1930, Klein batted .386, hit 40 homers, and drove in 170 runs—but didn't lead the league in any of those categories, although he was tops in runs (158) and doubles (59).

His RBI and doubles totals still rank as the best in Phillies history, as does his .687 slugging percentage that year. In 1931 he led the league in homers, RBI, and runs, and was named most valuable player by *The Sporting News*. One year later he won BBWAA Most Valuable Player honors while leading in runs, hits, homers, stolen bases, and slugging. In 1933, he won the Triple Crown with 28 homers, 120 RBI, and a .368 average but finished second to Giants hurler Carl Hubbell in the MVP voting.

Ed Delahanty, 1889

Sherry Magee, 1914

Johnny Moore was a .300-plus hitter in all four of his seasons with the Phils (1934–1937), with a high of .343 in 1934. Morrie Arnovich (1936–1940) earned a trip to the All-Star Game in 1939, when he batted .324, although he did not see any action in the annual midseason exhibition.

Danny Litwhiler was a standout outfielder during the Phils' bleakest era of the early 1940s, leading the team with 18 homers in 1941 while batting .305. He singled in the lone All-Star Game at bat of his career, in 1942. Ron Northey went .288–22–104 in 1944 and later was traded to the Cardinals for Harry Walker, who proceeded to lead the league in hitting in 1947 with a .363 average.

Del Ennis went from Rookie of the Year in 1946 to league RBI champ and a cornerstone of the Whiz Kids pennant winners in 1950. In 11 seasons with Philadelphia, he hit above .300 three times, knocked 25 or more home runs seven times, and drove in more than 100 runs in six seasons. He is second on the Phillies' all-time list in home runs with 259 and third in RBI.

Almost simultaneous to Ennis' emergence, Richie Ashburn was building Hall of Fame credentials. The 1948 Rookie of the Year, he went on to win two batting titles and hit over .300 in 8 of 12 seasons with the Phillies. When Ashburn won his second batting crown in 1958 with a .350 average, he also led the league with 215 hits, his third season above the 200 mark. Ashburn is second only to Mike Schmidt among Phillies career leaders in games, at bats, and hits; he also ranks third in runs scored.

Cy Williams and Chuck Klein, circa 1928

Johnny Callison, Sports Illustrated *cover, August 10, 1964*

Greg Luzinski, 1975

Maddox, the "Secretary of Defense," was known more for his glove work, earning seven straight Gold Glove awards, but he was also a career .285 hitter and once batted as high as .330 (1976).

Jay Johnstone was the third piece of the outfield from 1975 to 1977, during which time he batted .310. Bake McBride joined the mix midway through the 1977 season and stayed through 1981. He batted .309 for the 1980 world champs and, with Maddox, was a base-stealing threat. Gary "Sarge" Matthews was a fine hitter who hit .301 in 1981 and was the MVP of the 1983 NLCS with 3 homers, 8 RBI, and a .429 batting average in the four games.

During the mid-1980s, the Phillies outfield featured Glenn Wilson (1984–1987), who earned an All-Star Game invitation in 1985 while leading the team with 102 RBI; Von Hayes (1983–1985, 1989–1991), who stole 202 bases and hit 124 homers in nine seasons with Philadelphia, including three as the first baseman; and the speedy Milt Thompson, who manned center field for three seasons (1986–1988) before being traded to St. Louis, only to re-sign with the Phillies in 1993, just in time to play for the pennant winners.

Two other outfielders on the World Series team in 1993 were Lenny Dykstra and Jim Eisenreich. After being traded from the Mets in June of 1989, Dykstra hit a career-high .325 in 1990 and led the National League in on-base percentage (.418). In 1993 he sparked the Phils to the pennant with league-leading totals in hits (194), walks (129), and runs scored (143). He finished second to Barry Bonds in the MVP voting. Eisenreich, who battled through his bout with the neurological disorder Tourette's syndrome to achieve a 15-year major league career, batted over .300 in all four of his seasons with the Phillies (1993–1996), including a .361 mark in 1996.

Bobby Abreu hit over .300 six times, played in two All-Star Games, and won a Gold Glove Award during his nine-year Phillies tenure (1998–2006). Pat Burrell averaged 27 homers and 91 RBI in his nine seasons as a Phillies outfielder (2000–2008). In 2002 he hit 37 homers and drove in 116 runs while batting .282, and three seasons later he posted nearly identical numbers (32, 117, .281).

In addition to Burrell, the outfield of the 2008 World Series team included Shane Victorino and Jayson Werth. Victorino had the best season of his early career, hitting .293 and scoring 102 runs. Werth contributed 24 home runs and stellar fielding in what was his second season with the Phils. In 2009, with the free-agent departure of Burrell, Werth and Victorino were joined by Raul Ibañez. That July, all three Phillies outfielders were named to the National League all-star team, Ibañez and Victorino as starters and Werth as a reserve.

From 1960 to 1969, Johnny Callison was a clutch hitter who knocked double-figure home runs in eight seasons, with a high of 32 in 1965, and collected at least 10 triples every year from 1961 to 1965. Callison's outfield mate through most of the 1960s was Tony Gonzalez, a .295 hitter in nine seasons with the Phillies.

The next decade and through the team's Golden Era, the outfield was anchored primarily by Greg Luzinski and Garry Maddox. Luzinski, known as "The Bull," hit at least 18 homers in each of his eight full seasons in Philadelphia, with a high of 39 in 1977. He led the league in RBI in 1975 with 120, although his career high was 130 in 1977. Luzinski also batted over .300 three times (1975–1977).

Left: *Lenny Dykstra, 1993 World Series*

Below: *Pat Burrell, 2008 World Series*

Phillies hitters have won nine batting championships. Seventeen different players have collected 200 or more hits in a season, and eight of them did it more than once. One time, the Phillies had four players bat over .400 in the same season. On four other occasions, three of the National League's top five hitters were Phillies.

Within a few years of the team's inception, the Phillies were fielding lineups with great hitters. In 1890, three players—Billy Hamilton, Jack Clements, and Sam Thompson—all placed in the top five of the league batting race. The next year, Hamilton won the team's first batting crown (.340). He repeated as batting king in 1893 (.380), while Thompson (.370) finished second and Ed Delahanty (.368) third in the league. Hamilton finished among the NL's top five hitters in each of his six seasons with Philadelphia.

Delahanty, one among five baseball-playing brothers, was a career .346 hitter (.361 with Philadelphia) who topped the .300 mark in 10 straight seasons. In 1894, the all–Hall of Fame outfield of Delahanty, Hamilton, and Thompson, plus reserve outfielder Tuck Turner, staged one of the most incredible years in baseball history when all four hit above .400—although all trailed Hugh Duffy's .440 with Boston. As a team, the Phils batted .349. The following year, Delahanty again batted over .400, finishing second in the league, while Clements and Thompson finished third and fourth, respectively. Delahanty finally won a batting title in 1899 when he hit a career-best .410.

By then, with Hamilton traded and Thompson retired, three more outstanding hitters had joined the lineup. Nap Lajoie batted .345 in his five seasons with the Phillies (1896–1900), and Elmer Flick was a .338 hitter in four seasons (1898–1901). Neither batted lower than .302 in any season. Roy Thomas averaged .310 from 1899 to 1905.

Sherry Magee won a batting crown in 1910 with a .331 average, one of five seasons over .300. His place as a high-average batsman was taken in the 1920s by Cy Williams, a six-time .300

Elmer Flick, circa 1892

Sherry Magee, 1911

hitter, backed by Fred Leach, a .300-plus hitter in four seasons as a regular. While the team was imbedded in a long era of losing, Lefty O'Doul won the batting title in 1929 with a .398 average—the highest single-season average by a post-1900 Phillies hitter. That year, while reaching base 334 times (including 76 walks and 4 times hit-by-pitch), O'Doul set an NL record with 254 hits.

Losing records and strong hitting continued over the next few years, exemplified by a team average of .315 in 1930, the third-highest mark in National League history (post-1900). Five starters hit over .300: Chuck Klein (.386), O'Doul (.383), Pinky Whitney (.342), Don Hurst (.327), and Spud Davis (.313); utility man Bernie Friberg hit .341. The team still finished in last place, 40 games out.

Between 1929 and 1933, Klein mounted the best first five seasons of any player in baseball history. After playing 64 games in 1928, he hit as high as .386 and no lower than .337 while

Chuck Klein, 1930

Richie Ashburn, en route to a batting title, 1958

collecting 200 or more hits in each of his first five full seasons. His cumulative average from the time of his major league debut in July 1928 through his Triple Crown season of 1933 was .359.

Johnny Moore hit a career-high .343 in his first season with the Phillies (1934) and posted a .329 average over his four years in Philadelphia. In 1947, Harry Walker hit .363 to bring home the first Phillies first batting crown since Klein in 1933.

Richie Ashburn wielded the team's hottest bat from the late 1940s to the late 1950s. He won two batting crowns (.338 in 1955 and .350 in 1958), finished second twice, and collected more than 200 hits three times. His 1958 batting title was the last one for a Phillies player.

During the 1960s, Dick Allen batted .311 over his first four seasons (1964–1967), and Tony Gonzalez topped .300 three times in the decade, finishing second in the league in 1967 (.339). Garry Maddox (.330 in 1976) and Pete Rose (.331 in 1979) were the only Phillies to finish among the NL's top hitters during the 1970s. Rose was wearing a Phillies uniform when he passed Stan Musial as the all-time National League hits leader in 1981.

Lenny Dykstra, John Kruk, and Jim Eisenreich gave the Phillies consistently high averages in the 1990s. Eisenreich never batted below .300 in four seasons with the Phillies, and Kruk topped the mark in four out of six seasons, batting .309 in his career as a Phillie.

Bobby Abreu continued the trend in the early 2000s, with six .300-plus seasons between 1998 and 2004. Ultimately, the hitting badge of excellency has been turned over to Chase Utley, who finished third in the league with a .332 average in 2007 and has ably followed in the path of past Phillie greats.

Pete Rose, 1983

Bobby Abreu, 2005

Chase Utley, 2009

HOME RUN KINGS

The Phillies have seldom been without big home run hitters on the roster. Going back to the early days, the club has almost always had someone who could regularly poke the ball over the fence.

From Sam Thompson and Ed Delahanty to Gavvy Cravath and Cy Williams; from Chuck Klein to Del Ennis to Dick Allen; from Greg Luzinski and Mike Schmidt to Scott Rolen, Jim Thome, Pat Burrell, and on up to Ryan Howard, some of the finest long-distance clouters in baseball have graced the Phillies lineup. Among them, this group has led or tied for the National League lead in home runs 27 times.

It's helped, of course, that most of the time the Phillies have played in hitter-friendly ballparks. At different times, Baker Bowl was 270 to 280 feet down the right-field line, and although a high wall stood in the way, left-handed swingers could easily pop balls onto the adjacent Broad Street. Both Shibe Park and Veterans Stadium, with their not-too-distant outfield walls, were also conducive to hitters who could swat the long ball. And Citizens Bank Park has quickly built a reputation as a place where hitters can easily smack long drives that fly, as Harry Kalas used to say, "outta here."

Gavvy Cravath, circa 1915

Mike Schmidt, 1980

Schmidt, the team's longest tenured player, is the all-time home run leader. He spent his entire career with the club and, over the course of 18 years (1972–1989), hit 548 homers—more than double the total of the next-best Phillie. Schmidt won or shared eight home run titles and hit more home runs (313) than any other major leaguer during the decade of the 1980s. His personal single-season high—and before the arrival of Howard, the club single-season record—was 48 dingers in 1980. He hit 30 or more home runs in a season 14 times and hit two or more homers in a game 44 times, both franchise records.

He also hit some particularly memorable blasts. On April 17, 1976, Schmidt hit four home runs against the Chicago Cubs, including the game-winner in the 10th inning, as the Phillies overcame a 12–1 deficit to win, 18–16. Three years later, again against the Cubs, his 10th-inning homer was the deciding blow in a 23–22 slugfest on May 17, 1979. In 1980 Schmidt delivered an 11th-inning clout to give the Phillies a 6–4 victory over the Montreal Expos and clinch the East Division title. In 1981, Schmidt's 10th-inning blast led the National League All-Stars to a 5–4 victory in the midseason classic.

Del Ennis, 1946

Sam Thompson, 1889

Dick Allen, circa 1964

Among other Phillies home run kings, Cravath is next in line with his five outright titles plus one tie between 1912 and 1919. Although he doesn't rank among the all-time leaders, Cravath was the premier home run hitter of his day. In 1915, when he hit a career-high 24, it marked the highest total in the major leagues to that point in the twentieth century, and it stayed that way until Babe Ruth eclipsed it in 1919.

Del Ennis spent 11 seasons with the Phillies and ranks second on the club's all-time list with 259 homers. Twice, he hit 30 or more homers in a season, although he never finished among the top three home run sluggers in the National League in any season.

The Philadelphia lineups of the previous century featured several home run threats as well. Sam Thompson's 20 homers in 1889 not only led the league but also stood as the major league single-season record until 1899. Thompson won another league crown in 1895 with 18. Future Hall of Famer Ed Delahanty led the NL in 1893 with 19 homers and, in 1896, became the first Phillies player to hit 4 home runs in one game.

Cy Williams won his first of three home run titles as a Phillie in 1920 (15) and three years later established a new National League record with 41 homers. He tied for another title in 1927 with 30.

In the late 1920s and early 1930s, Chuck Klein won four home run crowns while with the Phillies and ranks fourth on the franchise list with 243 total. After topping the league with a career-high 43 homers in 1929, Klein then won three straight titles from 1931 to 1933; his 40 homers in 1930 were only good enough for second best in the league. In July 1936, Klein became the first National Leaguer in the twentieth century to hit 4 home runs in one game.

After Klein, no Phillies hitter won a home run title until Schmidt came on the scene 40 years later, but that isn't to say the team was devoid of sluggers. Johnny Callison, who led the team every year from 1963 to 1965 while averaging 29 homers over that span, hit a memorable three-run clout in the bottom of the ninth inning of the 1964 All-Star Game to give the National League a 7–4 victory.

Jim Thome, 2005

Ryan Howard, 2009

In 1966, Dick Allen, who in his prime wielded a 42-ounce bat, became the first Phillie since Klein in 1930 to hit 40 homers in one season. Allen is also generally considered to have hit the longest home run in team history, a 529-foot monster that rocketed over the left-field roof at Connie Mack Stadium, over a row of houses across Somerset Street, and was found in a driveway behind the houses.

Greg Luzinski hit 223 homers for the Phillies and was Schmidt's main slugging partner during the 1970s. He hit a career-best 39 in 1977, one more than Schmidt that year.

A long drought of home run kings followed Schmidt's retirement, until Jim Thome came to town in 2003 and hit 47 homers to win the NL crown. He followed with 42 in 2004. Prior to Thome, Bobby Abreu, Pat Burrell, and Scott Rolen were the team's main long-ball threats. Burrell reached 30 homers in four different seasons and ranks third all-time on the franchise list (251).

In recent years, a new home run king has emerged. If he keeps his current pace, Ryan Howard may well become the Phillies' all-time greatest power hitter. No one in major league history has reached 100 career home runs faster than Howard, who hit the benchmark in his 325th game; career homer number 200 came in his fifth full season. Howard has already set the club record for most home runs in one season (58 in 2006), and in 2009 he broke the franchise record for career grand slams with number 8. In 2009, Howard, Chase Utley, Jayson Werth, and Raul Ibañez became the first Phillies quartet to each hit 30 or more homers in the same season.

Despite all of these formidable home run hitters who've worn the uniform of the Phillies, none of them can claim to have hit the greatest home run in team history. That honor goes to Dick Sisler, whose father, Hall of Famer George Sisler, watched from the stands when his son hit his memorable blast. Not particularly noted as a home run hitter—he never hit more than 13 in one season—Sisler's three-run shot in the 10th inning on the final day of the 1950 season gave the Phillies a 4–1 victory over the Dodgers and their first pennant in 35 years.

SPEED MERCHANTS

Speed alone is not enough to get a ticket to the big leagues, but in a game where players are scouted on their all-around abilities, it helps to be fast. A player who can use his speed to get on and around the bases brings an important dimension to a team's offense.

The Phillies' first successful stolen base artist was Jim Fogarty, an outfielder in the 1880s. Fogarty registered 102 steals in 1887 and led the National League with 99 in 1889. Just two years later, he died of tuberculosis at the age of 27.

Billy Hamilton, one of the team's all-time hitters, was also a leading speed merchant in the 1890s. While with the Phillies, Sliding Billy led the league in swipes four times. After stealing a league-high 102 bases in 1890, Hamilton's 115 thefts in 1891 set a major league record that stood until Lou Brock broke it in 1974.

Hamilton retains the franchise single-season record. In 1894, he tied a major league record that still stands with 7 steals in one game. Only two players—Brock and Rickey Henderson—stole more bases in a career than Hamilton, whose 508 steals tops the Phillies' all-time list.

In the years that followed, Ed Delahanty—who pilfered 58 sacks in 1898 and is the Phillies' second-highest all-time stealer with 412—Roy Thomas, and Sherry Magee became the club's top base-stealers. Magee, who once stole home twice in one game and twice swiped four sacks in a single contest, led the team six times.

One Phillies speedster earned distinction for another reason. Hans Lobert, the third baseman from 1911 to 1914, once raced a horse around the bases. Lobert was leading as the two

Richie Ashburn, circa 1950

Juan Samuel, circa 1986

rounded second base but was nudged by the nag and dropped behind. The third baseman lost by a nose. Lobert did lead the Phillies in stolen bases three times in his four seasons.

Stolen bases eventually became less popular, particularly after Babe Ruth and others made the long ball the focus of attention. By 1932, Chuck Klein's 20 steals were enough to lead the league. In 1941, Danny Murtaugh was first in the NL with 18 stolen bases.

In 1948, Richie Ashburn brought his speed to the Phillies and, starting as a rookie when he led the league with 32 steals, reigned for more than a decade as the club's top stolen-base artist. He led all teammates in steals in 11 of 13 seasons.

Tony Taylor led the Phils in steals five times in the 1960s, and Larry Bowa took over in the 1970s, topping the squad six times. Juan Samuel, one of the fastest runners the Phillies have ever had, dominated the 1980s. In 1984, he pilfered 72 sacks, the highest Phillies total since Hamilton swiped 97 bases in 1895. That year, Samuel teamed with Von Hayes (48) and

Jeff Stone (27) for a total of 147 steals, the highest total for a Phillies threesome since the Hamilton-Delahanty-Thompson trio stole 170 in 1895.

Lenny Dykstra was the club's leading base-snatcher every year from 1989 through 1995, with a high of 37 in 1993. Later, Doug Glanville and Bobby Abreu earned their places as leading speedsters.

Since his rookie season of 2001, when he tied for the league lead with 46 steals, Jimmy Rollins has been the reigning speed merchant. A smart and cunning base-runner, Rollins has combined these assets with quickness to average 36 thefts in his first nine full seasons while succeeding on 83 percent of his attempts. He already ranks among the top four all-time base stealers in team history.

In recent years, Rollins has been joined by Shane Victorino and Jayson Werth as players who dash on the base paths with outstanding speed. In his first four seasons in Philadelphia, Victorino stole more than 100 bases.

Jimmy Rollins, 2009

Garry Maddox, Mike Schmidt, Larry Bowa, and Bob Boone, 1978 Gold Glove Award winners

DEFENSIVE STANDOUTS

I t was once said that two-thirds of the Earth was covered by water, and the other third was covered by Garry Maddox. Such a proclamation not only provided testimony to the magnificent defensive play of the Phillies' center fielder, but it also suggested the vital importance placed on the art of fielding baseballs.

For any team, fielding baseballs successfully is a necessary part of winning games. The landscape is cluttered with teams heavily stocked with defensive bunglers. Paint such teams losers.

On the other hand, find a team richly endowed with skillful glove men, and there's a good chance that team is a winner. The 2008 Phillies team is a perfect example.

Shortstop Jimmy Rollins (.988) and center fielder Shane Victorino (.994) won Gold Gloves. Pedro Feliz (.974) finished second among third basemen, and Chase Utley (.984) finished third among second basemen in fielding percentage. Catcher Carlos Ruiz (.993), left fielder Pat Burrell (.991), and right fielder Jayson Werth (.992) also played outstanding defense. What better way to help win a championship than to have a lineup stocked with players who can catch the ball?

The 1980 champs made the same point. Maddox (.976) and Mike Schmidt (.946) won Gold Gloves. First baseman Pete Rose fielded .997. Right fielder Bake McBride (.990), second baseman Manny Trillo (.987), and shortstop Larry Bowa (.975) were among the league leaders in fielding percentage at their positions.

Bowa has the highest career fielding percentage (.980) for a shortstop in National League history. Schmidt won 10 Gold Gloves, Maddox captured 8, and Trillo, owner of one of the strongest arms of any second sacker in baseball, grabbed 3. The Phillies' best teams have not bobbled many balls.

Since the Gold Glove Award was introduced in 1963, the Phillies have won 41 times. Third baseman Scott Rolen earned three, while Bowa, Boone, pitcher Jim Kaat, and Rollins won two apiece.

Outstanding glove men have been a staple of Phillies lineups dating back to the 1880s. In 1886, first baseman Sid Farrar and second baseman Charlie Bastian led the National League in fielding percentage. First basemen Willard Brown (1891) and Roger Connor (1892), third baseman Lave Cross (1895), and outfielders Jim Fogarty (1889) and Sam Thompson (1894, 1896) also won fielding titles before the turn of the century.

In later years, many other Phillies led the league in fielding percentage. Bowa in the 1970s and third baseman Willie Jones in the 1950s finished tops at their respective positions five times. Third baseman Harry Wolverton (1901, 1903, 1904), catcher Bill Killefer (1913, 1916, 1917), third baseman Pinky May (1939, 1941, 1943), and center fielder Tony Gonzalez (1962, 1964, 1967) each led three times as well.

Charlie Bastian, with Pop Schriver, 1888

Larry Bowa making the tag, with Manny Trillo backing up, 1979

Right fielder Jim Fogarty, 1887

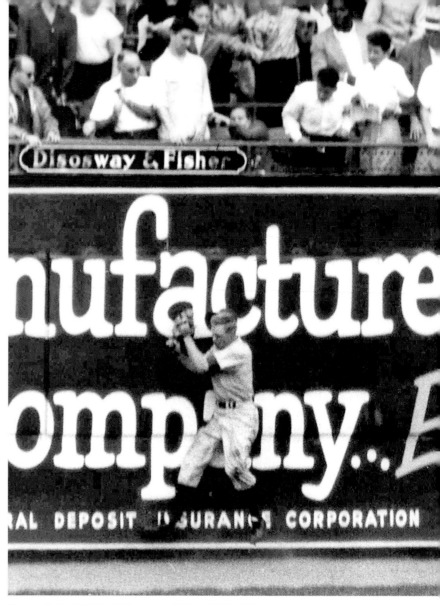

Center fielder Richie Ashburn, at Ebbets Field, 1953

Right fielder Chuck Klein set a modern major league record in 1930 when, aided by the short right field at Baker Bowl, he registered 44 assists. It was one of three times that Klein led NL outfielders in assists. Right fielder Johnny Callison led the league in outfield assists four times, while center fielder Richie Ashburn and right fielder Gavvy Cravath each did it three times.

Ashburn, of course, made the greatest outfield throw in Phillies history when he nailed the Brooklyn Dodgers' Cal Abrams at the plate in the bottom of the ninth inning of the last game of the 1950 season. Instead of it being the winning run for the Dodgers, the Phils went on to victory an inning later to clinch the pennant.

Ashburn holds major league records for most years leading the league in putouts (nine), most years with 500 or more putouts (four), and most years with 400 or more putouts (nine). Schmidt holds National League records for most assists in a career (5,045), most assists in a season (404), and most years (tied with Ron Santo) leading the league in assists (7) among third basemen

In 1942, left fielder Danny Litwhiler became the first major league outfielder to play in more than 150 games and field a perfect 1.000. Litwhiler went on to play in 187 consecutive games without making an error. Since then, Phillies outfielders Gonzalez (1962), Don Demeter (1963), Callison (1968), Milt Thompson (1994), Jim Eisenreich (1995), and Victorino (2006) have all had 1.000 seasons, although none played as many as 150 games in the outfield. Ron Northey, Glen Gorbous, Bob Bowman, Ken Walters, Ollie Brown, Mike Anderson, Joe Lefebvre, Glenn Wilson, and most recently Victorino and Werth were also all known for their strong throwing arms from the outfield.

Center fielder Garry Maddox, at Dodger Stadium, 1978 NLCS

Center fielder Shane Victorino, at Citizens Bank Park, 2008 NLCS

Numerous other Phillies players have special fielding accomplishments. In 1946, first baseman Frank McCormick made just one error while playing in 134 games. In 1982, Trillo accepted 479 consecutive chances (89 games) without an error. In 1999, catcher Mike Lieberthal played in 145 games and posted a fielding percentage of .997, committing just three errors.

Phillies fielders have turned 32 triple plays since the first one was achieved in 1890. The Phils reeled off three tri-killings in 1964. Shortstops Heinie Sand and Bobby Wine each participated in three triple plays. The team's greatest triple play came in 1992 when second baseman Mickey Morandini turned one unassisted. He was only the second player at his position in baseball history to accomplish that feat. Against the Mets on August 23, 2009, reserve second baseman Eric Bruntlett became only the second player in major league history to end a game with an unassisted triple play.

On the flip side of the coin, the Phillies once made an improbable three errors on the same play. In a 1942 game against the Reds, second baseman Albie Glossop threw wildly to first after fielding Gee Walker's grounder. First baseman Nick Etten retrieved the ball but threw it away trying to catch Walker at third. Despite the wild throw, third baseman Pinky May wasn't on the bag anyway, so he was charged with an error as Walker raced home.

Among the other outstanding defensive Phillies are catchers Darren Daulton, Spud Davis, Jimmie Wilson, and Andy Seminick; first basemen Rico Brogna, Eddie Waitkus, Bill White, and Willie Montanez; second basemen Dave Cash, Tony Taylor, and Emil Verban; third basemen Don Money and Pinky Whitney; shortstops Dick Bartell and Dave Bancroft; outfielders Lenny Dykstra, Ethan Allen, and Dode Paskert; and pitchers Grover Cleveland Alexander, Rick Wise, Eppa Rixey, and Robin Roberts.

STARTING PITCHERS

No player on the baseball diamond is more intensely scrutinized than the starting pitcher. His every move is watched and subsequently analyzed by nearly everybody in the ballpark. A starter is the center of attention, whether his pitching is good or bad.

Of course, there are all kinds of starting pitchers. There are thin ones and short ones, tall ones and chubby ones. Some throw hard, some throw soft. Some are mean, some are cunning, some are easy-going. There is no set formula for the model starter, but his importance to his team is limitless. As the venerable tactician Connie Mack once said, "Pitching is 75 percent of the game."

The Phillies have had flingers of every stripe, but three in particular give credence to Mack's theory. Grover Cleveland Alexander, Robin Roberts, and Steve Carlton stand far atop the pyramid of Phillies pitchers. All are members of the Hall of Fame. Alexander and Carlton each won more than 300

Grover Cleveland Alexander, 1913

Robin Roberts, circa 1950

games in their careers, and Roberts won 286. All pitched their teams to pennants—a rare accomplishment in Phillies annals. Collectively, they won 20 or more games 17 times. Although none of the three fired a no-hitter, Alexander and Carlton each registered six one-hitters, and Roberts pitched three.

Phillies pitchers made news right from the start. In the club's first year in 1883, there was one principal starter, John Coleman. With a 12–48 mark, he set records that still stand in losses, hits (809), and runs (544) while starting 61 of the team's 97 games, completing 59, relieving in 4 others, and working 538 innings. The team's second hurler that year, Art Hagan, started 16 games and lost 14 of them.

The following season, as the Phillies improved considerably from their 17–81 debut, a new pitcher of note emerged. Charlie Ferguson won 99 games over the next four years, including 30 in 1886, one year after he gave the Phillies their first of nine no-hitters. During spring training in 1888, Ferguson was stricken with typhoid fever and died at the age of 25. A whole city mourned his passing.

Twenty-game winners were much more plentiful on the abbreviated staffs of early baseball teams. Along with Ferguson, Phillies pitchers won 20 or more games 24 times during the 1800s, including 38 by Kid Gleason in 1890 and 32 by Gus Weyhing in 1892. Charlie Buffinton (1887–1889) and

Steve Carlton, 1982

Charlie Ferguson, circa 1887

Eppa Rixey, with Erskine Mayer in the background, 1913

Jack Taylor (1894–1896) each passed the 20 mark in three consecutive seasons. Three-hundred-game-winner Tim Keefe closed out his Hall of Fame career with two and a half years in Philadelphia, winning 19 games with a 2.36 ERA in 1892. Kid Nichols, another Cooperstown inductee and 300-game winner, also spent the final seasons of his career in a Phillies uniform.

Red Donahue pitched a no-hitter in 1898, and a year later he was one of three 20-game winners on the staff, along with Chick Fraser and Wiley Piatt. Donahue won 20 games in 1901, as did Bill Duggleby and Al Orth. Tully Sparks emerged as a strong starter a couple of years later, going 22–8 with a 2.00 ERA in 1907. Two more no-hitters were fired by Phillies in the opening decade of the new century, by Fraser in 1903 and John Lush in 1906. When Grover Cleveland "Pete" Alexander joined the team in 1911, the Phillies got their first glimpse of real greatness on the mound.

Staging the finest rookie season of any big league pitcher, Alexander won 28 games, at one point hurling four straight shutouts. He then recorded 68 more victories over the next three seasons before pitching the 1915 Phils to the pennant with 31 wins, 4 of which were one-hitters. That year he claimed the pitching Triple Crown, leading the league in wins, ERA, and strikeouts. He was also tops in complete games and shutouts. Ol' Pete won another Triple Crown the following year, in one of the greatest seasons baseball has ever seen: 33 wins, 38 complete games, 389 innings pitched, and an amazing total of 16 shutouts, an all-time major league record. Alexander hit 30 wins for a third straight season in 1917 and again led the National League in complete games, innings pitched, strikeouts, shutouts, and victories. Then the Phillies traded him to the Cubs. By the end of his career in 1930, Alexander had won 373 games, which ties him for the third most in baseball history. His 90 shutouts, 61 of them with the Phillies, are the second most of any pitcher.

Curt Simmons, circa 1960

Chris Short, circa 1966

Alexander was not the only elite hurler on the Phillies during the 1910s. Eppa Rixey kicked off his long journey to Cooperstown with eight seasons in Philadelphia, peaking with a 22-win season in 1916, and Erskine Mayer won 21 games in two consecutive seasons (1914–1915). By 1921, Alexander, Rixey, and Mayer were all gone, and good Phillies pitchers were scarce over the next three decades. Some years, the team's top pitcher won no more than eight or nine games. Ray Benge won in double figures four years in a row (1929–1932)—although he lost in double figures in every one of his five seasons in Philadelphia, making for a 57–78 record overall. While Benge was enjoying his best season in 1931 (14 wins, 3.17 ERA), Jumbo Jim Elliott tied for the league lead with 19 wins, on a team that went 66–88. As terrible teams proliferated, the Phils often traded away their best hurlers, including Curt Davis, Bucky Walters, Claude Passeau, and Kirby Higbe, all of whom went on to success elsewhere.

Veteran pitcher Dutch Leonard was purchased by the Phils after the 1946 season, and in each of the next two years he finished among the NL's top five pitchers in ERA, posting a 29–29 record over those two years. In 1948, Leonard and the staff were joined by the 21-year-old Robin Roberts.

Roberts went 7–9 in 20 starts as a rookie, improved to 15–15 as a sophomore in 1949, and then rattled off six consecutive seasons with 20 or more wins, including four in a row (1952–1955) as the National League's winningest pitcher. His 20th win in 1950 was the pennant-clincher. In 1952, he won 28 games and was named both Pitcher and Player of the Year by *The Sporting News*. Roberts led the league in complete games and innings pitched five years in a row, at one point completing an astounding 28 consecutive games, and was twice crowned strikeout king. He started an unprecedented five All-Star Games. His 234 wins and 1,871 strikeouts for the Phillies are second only to Carlton on the franchise leader board.

Right: *Jim Bunning, June 21, 1964*

John Denny, 1983

Curt Simmons spent 12 seasons with the Phillies (he missed 1951 while in military service) and won 115 games during that span. He received a $60,000 signing bonus as a teenager and went on to win 17 games for the 1950 Whiz Kids. He was the National League's starting pitcher in the All-Star Game in 1952 and 1957, meaning that from 1950 to 1957, a Phillies pitcher was the starter in seven of eight midsummer classics.

Jack Sanford was named Rookie of the Year in 1957, winning 19 games and striking out an NL-high 188 batters, but he was only around in Philadelphia for one more season. Ray Culp also started off with a bang, posting a 14–11 record and 2.97 ERA in his rookie season of 1963, but he never quite matched that debut performance.

Chris Short, a 20-game winner in 1966, is the Phils' fourth-highest winning pitcher, with 132 victories. Art Mahaffey set a club record in 1961 with 17 strikeouts in one game and notched 19 victories in 1962. The star pitcher of the decade, however, was Jim Bunning (1964–1967, 1970–1971), who posted three straight 19-win seasons. On June 21, 1964, he hurled the first perfect game in National League history. A year later he set a franchise record (since broken) with 268 strikeouts.

Rick Wise fired a no-hitter against Cincinnati in 1971—while becoming the first and to date only pitcher to hit two home runs in a game in which he hurled a no-hitter—and then was traded for Carlton after the season.

Curt Schilling, 1997

Cole Hamels, 2009

Steve Carlton's 329 wins rank him second in baseball history among left-handed pitchers, and he is one of only four pitchers to amass 4,000 strikeouts in a career. No pitcher in Phillies history has won more games or struck out more batters, and "Lefty" was the team's opening-day starter 14 times. He was a four-time Cy Young Award winner and seven-time all-star. He won 20 or more games five times and led the league in strikeouts five times. He was the ace on two pennant-winners, but his best performance came in a season in which the team won a mere 59 games. That year, 1972, Carlton posted career bests of 27 wins, 310 strikeouts, and a 1.97 ERA, becoming the only pitcher ever to win a Cy Young on a last-place team. Five years later, he won his second award as the Phils won a franchise-record 101 games.

When the Phillies won the NL pennant in 1983, righty John Denny was the team's top pitcher. With a 19–6 record and 2.37 ERA, Denny became the second Phillie hurler to claim a Cy Young Award. Reliever Steve Bedrosian added his name to the list, winning the Cy Young Award in 1987.

A decade later, the Phillies returned to the World Series with Curt Schilling leading the staff. In his nine seasons in Philadelphia (1992–2000), he won in double figures five times and twice struck out more than 300 batters in a season, including a club-record 319 in 1997. Tommy Greene won 16 of 20 decisions in 1993, and Terry Mulholland, an all-star that season, went 12–9 and had a staff-best 3.25 ERA. Both Greene and Mulholland threw no-hitters during their Phillies careers, as did Kevin Millwood.

Cole Hamels was an all-star in 2007, his second season in the league, and finished the year 15–5 with a 3.39 ERA. In 2008, he won 14 games in the regular season and went 4–0 in the postseason, earning MVP honors in both the NLCS and the World Series. Lefty Jamie Moyer went 16–7 for the pennant winners in 2008, and that October he went on to become the oldest pitcher ever to start a World Series game. A year later, at age 46, he became the oldest big league hurler to reach 250 career wins.

RELIEF PITCHERS

In the modern game, a relief pitcher has become one of the most valuable members of a baseball team. That wasn't always the case.

In the early years of baseball, starters were expected to play the entire game—just as the other eight position players were—and it wasn't until about six decades ago that relievers took on a more consistent and useful function.

These days, to a large extent due to the heavy emphasis on pitch counts, relievers have ascended to an exalted level on every team's roster, and specialists abound. There are long relievers, middle-inning relievers, situation relievers, and set-up relievers, all followed by the ubiquitous closer.

Up until about the middle of the twentieth century, however, substitute pitchers were called in to "relieve" a struggling starter only in dire circumstances, and the men called in to put out the proverbial fire were typically washed-up hurlers or, occasionally, the ace of the team (if he wasn't starting), being the only one deemed reliable enough to stand on the mound. Indeed, in four different seasons, Grover Alexander finished among the league's top 10 in both complete games and saves. (His single-season high, however, was 3 saves, showing that the opportunities were few and far between.)

"Fidgety Phil" Collins was the first Phillie to lead the National League in saves (6 in 1933). In just over six seasons

"Fidgety Phil" Collins, early 1930s

Dick Farrell, 1958

Jim Konstanty, 1950

(1929–1935), he started 132 games for Philadelphia and came in to finish 96 others. Syl Johnson was another regular closer in the 1930s, and he twice finished among the league's top five in saves, with 7 his single-season high. In 1945, Andy Karl was the first Phillie to hit double-digit saves in a season when he posted a league-best 15 in a record-setting 67 appearances, all but 2 as a reliever.

When relievers gradually started taking on a more prominent role in team strategy, the Phillies were one of the first teams to jump on the bandwagon. The first heralded resident of the Phillies bullpen was Jim Konstanty, a well-traveled pitcher who had been mostly a starter before joining the team in 1948. Adapting quickly, Konstanty soon emerged as not only the Phillies' top fireman but one of the best among a small group of relievers in the major leagues.

A junkballer, the then-32-year-old Konstanty pitched in 53 games in 1949. The following season, he set a major league record with 74 appearances while winning 16 games and saving 22. That year, he was the most important reason the Phillies won the National League pennant, and as such he became the first reliever to win a Most Valuable Player award. Konstanty was named first on 18 of the 24 ballots while collecting 286 of a possible 336 points, easily beating out second-place Stan Musial. No reliever would win another MVP award until Rollie Fingers in 1981.

Although he had not started a single major league game in four years, Konstanty was named as the starting pitcher in the first game of the 1950 World Series—a choice necessitated by the exhausted state of the Phils' regular rotation. He lost a 1–0 decision to the New York Yankees, then pitched in relief in two other games during the four-game series.

Konstanty often worked multiple innings, in contrast to today's closers who seldom pitch more than one inning, and he once pitched eight innings in relief. His effectiveness diminished in later years—he was used often as a starter in 1953—and Konstanty was traded to the Yankees late in the 1954 season. After Konstanty, Dick "Turk" Farrell led the Phillies in saves more times (five) than any other reliever, accomplished in two different turns with the team (1957–1960, 1967–1969).

Just as Konstanty was a key figure in the 1950 pennant, each of the team's subsequent flag-holders had exceptional relief work: Tug McGraw in 1980, Al Holland in 1983, Mitch Williams in 1993, and Brad Lidge in 2008.

Tug McGraw, 1980 NLCS

Although McGraw, who pitched with the Phillies from 1975 through 1984, never led the league in saves, he saved 20 games in 1980 while posting a 1.46 ERA in 57 relief appearances. His 94 saves rank fourth on the franchise all-time list. During the 1970s, he formed a formidable bullpen trio with Gene Garber and Ron Reed.

Holland (1983–1985) was the Fireman of the Year during the 1983 pennant season, saving 25 games. Four years later, Steve Bedrosian brought home not only the Fireman award but also the Cy Young. His 40 saves were a league high and briefly stood as the single-season club record. That same season, 40-year-old Kent Tekulve set a team record with 90 appearances.

Bedrosian's save total was bested by Williams in 1993. Williams saved 43 regular-season games, but he's also remembered for serving up the home-run ball to Joe Carter that ended the World Series.

Jose Mesa, 2002

Brad Lidge, 2008 World Series

Jose Mesa claimed the single-season saves record among Phillies pitchers with 45 in 2002. Mesa, who also saved 42 games in 2001, holds the career franchise record of 112 saves, followed by Bedrosian (103), Williams (102), McGraw (94), and Reed (90).

In 2008, Lidge became the fourth pitcher in Phillies history to save 40 or more games in one season, and he did it in impressive fashion, saving 41 games in 41 opportunities. He also had a 1.95 ERA while appearing in 72 games. To illustrate the specialized role of closers in the modern game, in those 72 appearances he pitched a total of 69.1 innings—less than one inning per appearance. Lidge also saved 7 games in the postseason.

The long line of accomplished Phillies firemen also includes, Jack Baldschun (1961–1965), Dick Selma (1970–1973), Roger McDowell (1989–1991), Doug Jones (1994), Heathcliff Slocumb (1994–1995), Ricky Bottalico (1994–1988, 2001–2002), Mark Leiter (1998), Jeff Brantley (1999–2000), Billy Wagner (2004–2005), Tom Gordon (2006–2008), and Brett Myers (2007). All saved 20 or more games in at least one season, with Wagner (38), Bottalico (34 in 1996 and 1997), Slocomb, and Gordon all going over 30.

Rheal Cormier pitched in 84 games as a middle reliever in 2004, and Geoff Geary went 7–1 in 81 relief appearances in 2006. The 2008 Phillies bullpen had four pitchers appear in at least 70 games: J. C. Romero (81), Ryan Madson (76), Lidge (72), and Chad Durbin (71).

Among other noteworthy feats by Phillies relievers, Jones in 1994 and Slocumb in 1995 were back-to-back winners for the National League in the All-Star Game. Larry Andersen holds the team record for consecutive scoreless innings pitched by a reliever, with 33 in 1984. Jack Meyer (1958) and Willie Hernandez (1983) each own a share of the National League record for most consecutive strikeouts by a reliever with six.

OFF THE BENCH

As any big leaguer will attest, coming in off the bench is no easy job. But every team needs reserves who can enter a game, often on a moment's notice, and contribute something of value. On occasion, a reserve player will perform so well that they became regulars, while others spend their entire careers as backups.

Although the starting players generally were expected to play the entire game in the early days of baseball, reserves made important contributions nevertheless. The first significant reserve was Tuck Turner, who from 1893 to 1896 was a spare outfielder with a big bat. In 1894, when all three of the team's regular outfielders hit above .400, Turner batted .416. He added a .386 mark off the bench in 1895.

Fred Jacklitsch was a backup catcher who also took brief turns at first base, second base, third base, and the outfield during his seven years with the Phillies (1900–1902, 1907–1910). Infielder Bernie Friberg was a key reserve during most of his eight-year tenure in Philadelphia (1925–1932). In 1944, 16-year-old infielder Putsy Caballero became the youngest player in team history as he began eight years as mostly a backup. Infielder Cookie Rojas (1963–1969) played every position while performing part of his career as a reserve infielder. And in 1980, outfielder Lonnie Smith was named National League Rookie of the Year while hitting .339 in a part-time role.

Pinch hitters were also not a normal part of strategy in baseball's early years; the Phillies did not use a single pinch hitter until 1892, when Charlie Reilly got the team's first pinch hit. Soon enough, however, bringing in fresh batters "in a pinch" yielded significant contributions. Doc Miller slugged 20 pinch hits for the Phillies in

Cy Williams, circa 1926

Cookie Rojas, 1964

1913. Cy Williams holds the club record with nine pinch-hit home runs. In 1945, Vance Dinges clouted the team's only pinch inside-the-park home run. Dave Philley belted nine consecutive pinch-hits in 1958 and 1959. Gene Freese slugged five pinch-hit homers in 1959. Doug Clemens doubled in three straight games in 1967. Davey Johnson hit two pinch-hit grand slams in 1978.

The greatest pinch hitter in franchise history is Greg Gross, an all-around outfielder who from 1979 through 1988 collected 117 pinch-hits, a record far ahead of any other Phils pinch hitter. While accumulating a team record 461 at bats and 82 walks as a pinch-hitter, Gross led or tied for the team lead in pinch hits eight times. He had his finest hours as a pinch hitter during the 1980 NLCS, when he knocked three key hits to help the Phillies advance to the World Series.

Another top pinch-hitter of that era was outfielder Del Unser, who also delivered clutch hits in the 1980 postseason. He drove in the tying run and scored the winning tally in the ninth inning of the 4–3 win in Game Five of the World Series. One year earlier, he had recorded the unusual feat of belting pinch-hit home runs in three consecutive games.

Future Hall of Famers Dan Brouthers, Johnny Evers, Paul Waner, Jimmie Foxx, and Tony Perez all played reserve roles for the Phillies in brief stints with the team. Outfielders Glen Gorbous, Bob Bowman, and Ollie Brown had three of the strongest arms in Phillies history while manning backup posts. Infielders John Vukovich, Tommy Hutton, Kevin Jordan, and Tomas Perez; outfielders Dick Whitman, Jeff Stone, and David Delluci; and catchers Tim McCarver and Chris Coste also played key reserve roles.

One of the most successful role players the Phillies have ever had was picked up off waivers in 2007. During his first three seasons in Philadelphia, Greg Dobbs spent time at first base, third base, left field, and right field while also providing invaluable service as a pinch hitter. In 2008, Dobbs set team records with most hits (22) and most RBI (18) by a pinch hitter in one season.

Del Unser, 1980 NLCS

Greg Dobbs, 2008 NLCS

NICKNAMES

No statistic has yet been invented that ranks teams based on its nicknames. If it had been, the Phillies would surely place among the league leaders.

The Phils have seemingly had every nickname that the imagination could conjure. Some have been descriptive; some have been funny. And some have been, to say the least, downright curious.

The latter category would include nicknames such as Shucks (Hub Pruett), What's the Use (Pearce Chiles), Squack (Chester Crist), Wagon Tongue (Bill Keister), Klondike (Bill Douglas), She (Charles Donahue), and no doubt the leader of the pack, Death to Flying Things. That name, given to the Phillies' first manager and second baseman, Bob Ferguson, was said to describe either his ability to catch every ball hit his way or his penchant for nabbing all airborne bugs.

Other Phillies managers were bestowed with colorful nicknames as well. There was "Blondie" Bill Purcell, "Wild Bill" Donovan, Irving "Kaiser" Wilhelm, Pat "Whiskey Face" Moran, "Black Jack" Coombs, George "Stud" Myatt, Gene "The Little General" Mauch, Paul "Pope" Owens, and Terry "Tito" Francona.

More recently, the 2008 world champion Phillies featured JRoll (Jimmy Rollins), The Flyin' Hawaiian (Shane Victorino), Chooch (Carlos Ruiz), and Pat the Bat (Pat Burrell).

The 1993 pennant-winners took the field with Dutch (Darren Daulton), Nails (Lenny Dykstra), Head (Dave Hollins), Wild Thing (Mitch Williams), Jethro (Tommy Greene), Shills (Curt Schilling), and the Krukker (John Kruk). Players on other World Series teams included Ol' Pete (Grover Cleveland Alexander), Beauty (Dave Bancroft), Handle Hit (Milt Stock), Putt-Putt (Richie Ashburn),

"Death to Flying Things" Ferguson, circa 1883

"Puddin' Head" Jones and "Swish" Nicholson, 1949

Puddin' Head (Willie Jones), Bubba (Emory Church), Gnat (Larry Bowa), Whirlybird (Bob Walk), and Sarge (Gary Matthews).

Over the years, the Phillies have also fielded Ed "The Only" Nolan, Dirty Jack (Jack Doyle), Honest Jack (Jack Boyle), Fiddler (Frank Corridon), Phenomenal (John Smith), Little Poison (Lloyd Waner), Schoolboy (Linwood Rowe), and Crash (Dick Allen).

Pitchers have had descriptive nicknames like Losing Pitcher (Hugh Mulcahy), The Curveless Wonder (Al Orth), Weeping Willie (Claude Willoughby), Boom-Boom (Walter Beck), Fidgety Phil (Phil Collins), and Nibbler (Jim Hearn).

Phillies nicknames have paid particular attention to the animal kingdom. There was Possum (George Whitted), Tiger (Don Hoak), Bear (Jim Owens), Rabbit (Tom Glaviano and Jimmy Slagle), Mighty Mouse (Solly Hemus), Chicken (Nelson Hawks), Mule (John Watson), Hawk (Ken Silvestri), Squirrel (Roy Sievers), Turkey (Cecil Tyson), Donkey (Frank Thomas), Bull (Greg Luzinski), and last but hardly least, the Wild Elk of the Wasatch (Ed Heusser).

Ethnic or geographic references have also been popular, with names such as Greek (Bobby DelGreco), Chile (Jose Gomez), the Earl of Snohomish (Earl Torgeson), Irish (Mike Ryan), Bama (Carvel Rowell), and Tioga (George Burns). Going south, the Phils also had Palm Tree (Ron Stone) and Cactus (Gavvy Cravath).

The Phillies must have been good eaters, too. They had Apples (Andy Lapihuska), Peaches (George Graham), Peanuts (Harry Lowrey), Cookie (Octavio Rojas), Candy (John Callison), Beans (Harry Keener), Pickles (Bill Dillhoefer), Pretzels (John Pezzullo), Spud (Virgil Davis), Shad (Flint Rhem and John Barry), and Cod (Al Myers). Washing it all down was Whiskey Face (Pat Moran), Brewery Jack (John Taylor), and Buttermilk (Tommy Brown).

Some nicknames have focused on sartorial tastes. The team has seen Tight Pants (John Titus), Styles (Chris Short), High Pockets (Dick Koecher), and Bareback (Joe Oeschger). For their off-field exploits, there was Cupid (Clarence Childs) and the Charmer (George Zettlein).

The team has nurtured Smiling Al (Al Maul) and Mad Monk (Russ Meyer); Sleepy (Bill Burns) and Nap (John Shea); Cap (John Clark) and Harry the Hat (Harry Walker); and Iron Man (Wiley Piatt) and Rusty (Waldo Yarnall). There's also been Lucky (Jack Lohrke) and Jinx (Jennings Piondexter); Stretch (Howie Schultz) and Stumpy (Al Verdel); Hands (Chuck Hiller) and Stone Hands (Dick Stuart); Coonskin (Curt Davis) and Rawhide (Jim Tabor); Swats (Carl Sawatski) and Swish (Bill Nicholson); and Jumbo (Jim Elliott), Midget (Don Ferrarese), Bitsy (Elisha Mott), Runt (Jimmy Walsh), and Shorty (Glenn Crawford). Early in the twentieth century, John Titus was a Phillies outfielder whose nickname was

"Silent John." "He doesn't even make any noise when he spits," said teammate Kid Gleason.

During their existence, the Phillies have suited up at least 15 Lefties (the most prominent being Steve Carlton), about one dozen Reds, and various Kids, plus Kiddo (George Davis), Kitten (Harvey Haddix), and Kitty (Bill Bransfield and Jim Kaat).

In the front office, the Phillies have been presided over by Shetts (Billy Shettsline), Ruly (Robert R. M. Carpenter III), and Monty (David Montgomery). The Baron (Larry Shenk) directed public relations for 44 years. The Squire of Kennett Square (Herb Pennock) was once the general manager. And Maje (Robert McDonnell) served in various capacities with the team for more than 50 years.

"Nails" Dykstra, 1990

Comic Relief

Casey Stengel, 1920

From nimble-witted souls to frisky adventurers, Phillies rosters have almost always been dotted with specialists in comic relief. Many had a knack for saying funny things.

One of the club's all-time leaders in this category was the fun-loving reliever Tug McGraw. A first-rate comedian, McGraw had names for all his pitches. The Jameson—because Tug liked his whiskey hard and straight—was his fastball. Cutty Sark, with a label picturing a sailboat, was his curveball because it also sailed. The Peggy Lee—inspired by the singer's signature tune, "Is That All There Is?"—was his change-up. And because it had a nice tail on it, the Bo Derek was his slider.

In 1980, McGraw struck out Willie Wilson to end the final game of the World Series and bring the team the first championship in its 97-year history. Afterward, reporters asked Tug what kind of pitch he threw. "A fastball," he replied. "The slowest fastball in the history of baseball." "How do you figure that?" he was asked. "Because," said Tug, "it took 97 years to get there."

Several other colorful characters graced the Phillies dugout in the 1970s and 1980s. Jay Johnstone, a hugely popular player, often wore a cap with a pinwheel on the top. Relief pitcher Larry Andersen kept a collection of masks and wigs in his locker, including one that resembled manager Paul Owens. Once, after being booed unmercifully by the hometown fans, Mike Schmidt took the field for batting practice the next day wearing one of Andersen's long-haired wigs. The stunt effectively defused what had been an unpleasant situation. Schmidt once described Philadelphia as being "the only city where you can experience the thrill of victory and the agony of reading about it the next morning."

In 1921, the Phillies traded outfielder Casey Stengel to the New York Giants. When he heard the news while sitting half-dressed in the clubhouse during a rain delay, Stengel bolted through the door and onto the field where he circled the bases, sliding into each bag. Wet and covered with mud, Casey explained that he was celebrating his liberation from the then-woeful Phillies.

The Phillies pitching staff regularly got battered during the 1930s. On one occasion, second baseman and captain Fresco Thompson took the lineup card to the plate before the game. In the pitcher's spot, he had written, "Willoughby and others."

Complaining about the tiny hotel rooms Phillies players had to use on the road, pitcher Kirby Higbe said, "They were so small you had to go out into the hall to change your mind."

Tug McGraw, 1980

Whenever something went wrong on the mound, reliever Jim Konstanty summoned a friend who was an undertaker to come down from upstate New York and diagnose the problem. Konstanty also once encountered a fellow alumnus from Syracuse University. When asked if he remembered a particular classmate, Konstanty said he didn't. Informed that the person was a member of the ATO fraternity, Konstanty, who worked his way through college, said, "That lets me out. I was an IOU."

Tim McCarver was Steve Carlton's designated catcher through much of their years together with the Phillies. "When Lefty and I die," McCarver said, "they're going to bury us 60 feet, 6 inches apart."

Super slugger Dick Allen returned to the Phillies in the mid-1970s after the team had relocated to Veterans Stadium. Someone asked the first baseman how he liked playing on artificial turf as compared to grass. "Well," said Dick, "if a horse can't eat it, I don't like playing on it."

Infielder Davey Johnson, an avid reader, claimed he had read Leo Tolstoy's *War and Peace*. When some skeptics asked him to name the author, Johnson had the answer. "Of course, " he said, "it was Leo Toystore."

As the team bus passed Lake Michigan on its way from a downtown hotel to Wrigley Field in Chicago, outfielder Jeff Stone was curious. "Is that the Atlantic or the Pacific Ocean?" he asked. Another time, Stone turned down an offer of a shrimp cocktail. "No thanks," he said. "I don't drink." After playing in Venezuela in a winter league, Stone decided not to bring his newly purchased television home. Why? "Because they didn't speak anything but Spanish on it."

When a lady saw John Kruk eating a big meal, drinking a beer, and smoking during dinner at a New York restaurant, she was shocked. "How can an athlete have such bad habits?" she demanded. "I ain't an athlete, lady," Kruk replied, "I'm a baseball player." And in 1993 when it was said that the Phillies were a team of throwbacks to earlier times, Kruk responded, "We're throwbacks, all right. Thrown back by other organizations."

Phillies managers have had their share of witticisms. In 1888 after the Phillies had lost 14 of 19 games to the New York Giants, Harry Wright was asked to account for so many losses. "Those Giants," he said, "always seemed to finish with more runs."

In 1960, after managing the Phils to two straight last-place finishes in his second term as the team's skipper, Eddie Sawyer quit after the first game of the season. "I'm 49 and I want to live to be 50," he explained. Once when asked if his team had a morale problem, Danny Ozark assured listeners that, "Morality is not a factor on this team." And Larry Bowa urged a discontented player who claimed it was no fun playing with the Phillies, "If you want to have fun, go join a last-place team."

Jay Johnstone, 1978 NLCS

Mike Schmidt, 1985

ALL-STAR GAMES

Since the first All-Star Game in 1933, the Phillies have made some significant contributions to National League teams, including game-winning home runs, special pitching achievements, and a variety of other feats.

The most heralded feat came in 1964 when Johnny Callison slammed a three-run homer off Dick Radatz in the bottom of the ninth inning at Shea Stadium to give the National League a 7–4 victory. The blow, delivered with two outs, topped off a four-run inning for the winners. Callison was named the game's Most Valuable Player.

Another big Phillie blast came in 1981 at Cleveland when Mike Schmidt belted a two-run homer in the eighth inning against Rollie Fingers to give the Nationals a 6–4 victory. Dick Allen (1967) and Greg Luzinski (1977) also have homered for NL teams.

Johnny Callison hitting a home run, 1964 All-Star Game

Robin Roberts was the starting pitcher in a then-record five games (1950, 1951, 1953, 1954, 1955). With Curt Simmons starting in 1952 and 1957, Phillies pitchers opened seven games within an eight-year period. Steve Carlton (1979), Terry Mulholland (1993), and Curt Schilling (1999) also drew starting assignments in the midsummer classic. Bucky Walters, in 1937, was the first Phillie pitcher to make an all-star appearance. Three Phillies—Ken Raffensberger (1944), Doug Jones (1994), and Heathcliff Slocumb (1995)—have been winning pitchers, while Simmons (1957) and Art Mahaffey (second game, 1962) have each taken a loss.

Six Phillies managers have skippered National League teams. The first five—Eddie Sawyer (1951), Gene Mauch (1965), Dallas Green (1981), Paul Owens (1984), and Jim Fregosi (1994)—were on the winning side. Charlie Manuel's team lost in 2009.

In the first All-Star Game played in 1933 at Comiskey Park, Phillies shortstop Dick Bartell and right fielder Chuck Klein were both starters. In that contest, Klein became the first Phillies player to get a hit in an All-Star Game.

Schmidt has appeared in more all-star Games (12) than any Phillies player in history. Roberts and Carlton lead in games pitched with seven apiece. Larry Bowa was named to five all-star teams, and Chase Utley was the starting second baseman four straight times (2006–2009). Four Phillies—Bowa, Carlton, Schmidt, and Bob Boone—started in the 1979 game. The 2009 all-star roster featured five Phillies: Utley, Raul Ibañez, and Shane Victorino as starters, Ryan Howard and Jason Werth as reserves. It marked the fifth time in history that five Phils made the team in the same year; 1976, 1979, 1991, and 1995 are the others.

Philadelphia has played host to four All-Star Games. In 1943, Bobby Doerr's three-run homer gave the American League a 5–3 victory at Shibe Park. In 1952, Simmons and the Athletics' Bobby Shantz gave the city of Philadelphia starting pitchers on both teams. In the only All-Star Game ever stopped by rain, the Nationals claimed a 3–2 victory in five innings with the help of home runs by Jackie Robinson and Hank Sauer.

The 1976 game at Veterans Stadium saluted the nation's bicentennial with a crowd of 63,974 on hand to watch the Nationals prevail, 7–1. The NL won again, 6–0, when the All-Star Game returned to the Vet in 1996. Norristown native Mike Piazza of the Los Angeles Dodgers led the winners with a home run and double, earning him MVP honors.

Above: *Veterans Stadium,*
1996 All-Star Game

Left: *Ryan Howard and Raul*
Ibañez, 2009 All-Star Game

BALLPARKS

In a city that has had an abundance of noteworthy sports venues, Philadelphia's old baseball parks rank among the most prominent. Collectively, they are nearly as much a part of the city's rich baseball history as the teams themselves.

Stories about these old ballparks have been handed down from generation to generation. Grandfathers have told stories about going to Baker Bowl, fathers have recapped their days at Shibe Park, and their children have memories of Veterans Stadium and, more recently, Citizens Bank Park.

Altogether, the Phillies have called five different ballparks their home since the team began in 1883. Several other sites have been used as temporary quarters.

The early parks were all located in the North Philadelphia area of the city, while the last two were built in South Philly.

The first of the Phillies' ballparks was Recreation Park. Originally built in about 1860, the field had been used by various amateur teams before serving as an encampment for Union soldiers during the Civil War. Later, it was used by several Philadelphia professional teams, but by the late 1870s it had become rundown and was the site of a horse market.

When Al Reach learned in 1882 that he would be awarded a new franchise in the National League, he bought the park, cleared away the weeds, fixed up the field, and put in a grandstand that held 6,500 spectators. One year later, the first Phillies game was played there.

Recreation Park sat on an irregularly shaped city block bounded by Columbia and Ridge Avenues and 24th and 25th Streets. Although in a densely populated area now, the site was at the time considered to be on the outskirts of the city.

Despite its oddities, Recreation Park was the Phillies' home for four years, and the team compiled a 102–117–5 record there. But, as the Phils improved, the old ballpark became less able to accommodate the increasingly bigger crowds, and Reach decided to find a new home for his team.

Reach purchased property less than one mile away at Broad Street and Lehigh Avenue, where, at a cost of $101,000, he built a new ballpark on what was previously a dump. Originally called Philadelphia Base Ball Park or Huntingdon Street Grounds, the new park had 12,500 seats, had sheds for 55 horse-drawn carriages, and featured paneled brick and three turrets, one being 165 feet high. It was viewed as the finest stadium in the land.

The ballpark opened in 1887, and for the next 51½ years it was the Phillies' home. During that time, it housed the team's first World Series, was the home park of Hall of Famers such as

Aerial view of Baker Bowl

Aerial view of Shibe Park

Above: *Aerial view of Veterans Stadium*

Left: *Aerial view of Citizens Bank Park*

Right: *Recreation Park*

Below: *Baker Bowl, 1916*

Ed Delahanty, Billy Hamilton, Sam Thompson, Grover Cleveland Alexander, and Chuck Klein, and late in its life was even the first home of the Philadelphia Eagles.

Renamed Baker Bowl in 1913, the park was the scene of several major catastrophes. In 1894, a plumber's torch started a fire that resulted in the loss of much of the ballpark. The park was rebuilt with steel and a cantilever pavilion—both, at the time, new concepts in stadium construction—and with a seating capacity of 18,800. While the work was being done, the Phillies played on the University of Pennsylvania's baseball field.

Another major disaster occurred at Baker Bowl in 1903 when a balcony collapsed, dropping people 30 feet to the ground. Lured to the balcony by the shrieks of a group of young girls being accosted by two drunks outside the park, nearly 400 people fell. Twelve died and 232 were hospitalized. The Phillies were forced to move their games to Columbia Park, where the Philadelphia Athletics played.

Eventually, Baker Bowl, rundown and falling apart, became the laughing stock of baseball, derisively called a dump,

the "Toilet Bowl," and many more unflattering names. The Phillies moved out of the decrepit old ballpark in the middle of the 1938 season, having compiled an overall 1,957–1,778–29 record there.

Shibe Park at 21st Street and Lehigh Avenue, just seven blocks away from Baker Bowl, became the Phillies' next home. Opened in 1909 and owned and built at a cost of $315,248 by the Athletics, it was the first all-steel and concrete stadium in the nation. Its original capacity was 23,000, although over the years that was increased several times until it reached 33,608. (A doubleheader in 1947 with Jackie Robinson and the Brooklyn Dodgers attracted a record crowd of 41,660.)

The park had often played host to the Phillies over the years in City Series games with the Athletics and during a 12-game stretch in 1927 when a section of the stands had collapsed at Baker Bowl. After years of trying, Connie Mack had finally convinced the Phillies to abandon Baker Bowl and move to Shibe Park, which was named after the A's original majority owner, Benjamin Shibe.

Shibe Park, 1950

Veterans Stadium, April 2000

The site of eight World Series, including the Phillies' 1950 appearance, Shibe Park, with its green seats, green grass, and green walls, was also the site of the American League's first night game. It was the home of the Eagles for 18 years and of numerous Negro League games. Dick Allen and Del Ennis hit mighty home runs over the high roof in left field, and Robin Roberts and Richie Ashburn earned their Hall of Fame credentials there.

The name of the park was changed to Connie Mack Stadium in 1953, one year before the Athletics moved to Kansas City. The Phillies bought the park in 1954 for $1,657,000. In the ensuing years, though, the park aged badly and became surrounded by an increasingly dangerous neighborhood where drivers were obliged to pay to park their cars on the streets. The old ballpark finally became too obsolete to use. While fans took virtually everything they could pry loose, even including toilet seats, the Phillies played their last game there in 1970, concluding with a 1,205–1,415–13 record.

Dating back to 1953, the city had wanted to build a new stadium. After years of bickering, it finally happened when one was constructed at a cost of $52 million at Broad Street and Pattison Avenue in South Philadelphia. Named Veterans Stadium, it was a multipurpose venue that could be used for baseball and football.

Similar in design to other new stadiums of the era but considered superior because of its modern facilities, the Vet featured an AstroTurf playing field, had a giant electronic scoreboard, and was octagonal in shape. The seating capacity was 56,371 for baseball and 65,000 for football.

The Phillies played their first game there in 1971 before a crowd of 55,352. Over the ensuing years, the Vet gained notoriety for it pre-game entertainment, which included two 900-foot walks by the Great Wallenda across the top of the stadium on a high wire. It was also the birthplace of the widely heralded Phillie Phanatic and the site of Eagles and Army–Navy football games, as well as numerous other special events.

Citizens Bank Park, October 2008

Most of all, it was the stadium where the Phillies enjoyed some of their finest moments. The 1980 World Series ended at the Vet. Two other World Series were held there. Mike Schmidt hit 265 home runs and Steve Carlton won 138 games at the Vet. The Phils attracted crowds of more than two million in 14 different seasons, exceeding three million in 1993. And, playing at the Vet during their finest era, the Phillies posted a 1,414–1,199–3 record.

In its later years, the Vet became the subject of much criticism, some real, some imagined. The stadium often needed repairs, and over one period, the city spent $40 million for fixes. Early in 2004, Veterans Stadium was imploded. It took 62 seconds to destroy what had been a storied Philadelphia institution for 33 years.

That spring, the Phillies moved into Citizens Bank Park, which was built in an area that includes three other sports venues and is just down Pattison Avenue from where the Vet

stood. Costing $345 million, the stadium is strictly a baseball park with a grass infield and all the modern conveniences of a twenty-first-century ballpark. Exhibits celebrating the team's history, numerous places where fans can eat or drink along a long concourse, and elaborate facilities for the players help to make the ballpark one of the best, most attractive, and most fan-friendly in baseball.

CBP, which has developed a reputation as a hitters' park, has sections reaching as high as three levels, features a seating capacity of 43,674, and has parking in the area for 21,000 vehicles. Since it opened, it has averaged more than three million fans through its first six seasons, including a club-record 3,600,693 in 2009. A year earlier, the Phillies clinched the World Series at the park, setting off a massive round of festivities and, three days later, a parade that wound down Broad Street and ended with thousands of fans packing into the park for a jubilant celebration with the team. It was the perfect place to hold a party.

Clubhouse at Baker Bowl, circa 1938

DUGOUTS, CLUBHOUSES, AND BULLPENS

There was seldom anything normal about the Phillies' playing facilities. Especially in the early days, players had to deal with many unusual conditions.

For games at Recreation Park, the original home of the Phillies, players dressed in their rooms at a nearby hotel where they stayed, rode carriages to the field, and sat on benches in front of the stands. There were no such things as clubhouses or bullpens.

Conditions improved significantly when the team moved to Philadelphia Base Ball Park (later renamed Baker Bowl). Nothing fancy, but the ballpark did have a dugout, a clubhouse, and a bullpen.

Dugouts were small, cramped, and close to the fans. "We could sit in the dugout and smell the peanuts in the stands," pitcher Bucky Walters once said. Originally, the Phils' dugout was on the third-base side of the field, but manager Jimmie Wilson moved it across the diamond so he could be closer to the runners at first.

Clubhouse at Connie Mack Stadium, 1960s

Left: *Clubhouse at Veterans Stadium, 1996*

Below: *Clubhouse at Citizens Bank Park, 2005*

Grover Alexander and Pat Moran in front of dugout, Baker Bowl, October 1915

Pete Rose in dugout, Veterans Stadium, October 1980

Clubhouses were skimpy and located in center field. At first, there was only a Phillies clubhouse. Later, a second clubhouse was built atop it, and the Phils moved upstairs. Players had to walk across the field and up a flight of stairs to reach their lockers—or to use the bathroom during a game. Because both teams used the same stairs, fights were known to break out after games.

The locker rooms were bare bones at Baker Bowl. There were only two showers in the visitors' clubhouse and four in the Phillies'. The floors were wooden, and players hung their clothes on nails. "Each year, the club would give you a new nail," said pitcher Claude Passeau, who called the locker room "a hole in the wall."

The main feature of the Phillies' clubhouse in its early years was the presence of a swimming pool smack in the middle of the room. Players often jumped in after a game. Once, Hughie Jennings jumped in, and there was no water.

Baker Bowl's bullpens were located in front of the stands in foul territory beyond the dugouts. Players sat on benches so close to the stands that they could shake hands with the fans. Sometimes, warm-up throws bounced into the crowd.

Conditions improved after the Phils moved into Shibe Park (later renamed Connie Mack Stadium). Again, the bullpens were down the lines in foul territory, but they were blocked from the stands by high walls. The Phillies' bullpen was originally in left field, but manager Gene Mauch moved it to right so he could better see his pitchers warming up. Bullpen squatters could also wave towels to signal if a ball was going to hit the wall.

Ryan Howard entering dugout, Citizens Bank Park, October 2008

Dugouts were less than desirable at Shibe. "They were so deep you could hardly see the outfield or the bullpen," said Phils manager Eddie Sawyer. "You had to come out of the dugout to see well." But at least they were wide and spacious.

Shibe Park's clubhouse was small and very basic with metal lockers cramped closely together. In the home-team clubhouse (first used by the Athletics with the Phillies originally stationed in a much smaller area), a manager had his own office, and there were separate areas for trainers (in a loft overlooking the clubhouse) and equipment managers. Players had to walk from the clubhouse and across a thin corridor that was often populated with fans to reach a tunnel that led to the dugout.

The facilities continued to improve when the Phillies moved into Veterans Stadium. There, spacious bullpens were sealed off from the fans and located behind the walls in right and left fields. Dugouts sat slightly below field level and were wide enough to provide lots of room for a whole team.

The Phillies' clubhouse was large and surrounded by a variety of rooms, including training, dining, and equipment rooms; a manager's office; and a small locker room for the coaches. Lockers in the main clubhouse were sufficiently big that team leader Darren Daulton could fit a lounge chair in his, where he sat and presided over the rest of the team.

When the Phillies moved into Citizens Bank Park, the facilities got infinitely better. The sparkling, top-of-the-line, carpeted clubhouse features 44 lockers made of oak. Behind it is a room that includes 16 showers, a sauna, and a steam room. The clubhouse also contains numerous other rooms, including a doctors' office, a medical examination room, a video room, training rooms with 25 exercise machines, and a dining room and kitchen.

Elevated upper- and lower-level bullpens sit behind the center-field fence, with the Phillies using the bottom tier. Fans can get an overhead view of the bullpens from the outfield concourse. Huge dugouts accommodate the teams, and behind them are batting cages that are often used during games.

Bullpens at Citizens Bank Park, 2009

WALLS AND SCOREBOARDS

Among the many prominent and noteworthy features found in the various Phillies ballparks, the dimensions and scoreboards have been among the most distinctive.

Recreation Park, for instance, sat on an irregularly shaped city block that caused the outfield wall to sit only 300 feet from home plate down the left-field line and 331 feet to straightaway center. The wall then jutted out to 369 feet in right-center field before angling sharply back to 247 feet down the right-field line.

At both Baker Bowl and Shibe Park, the right-field walls were the focal points of a considerable amount of attention. The wall at Baker Bowl stretched across the outfield from right to dead center. Originally, it was 300 feet down the right-field line (341 to left and 408 to center), but to accommodate more seats behind the plate, it was shortened to 270. Later, foul territory was decreased, home plate was moved back, and the wall stood 280 feet, 5 inches away.

The wall was so close that sportswriter Red Smith, who covered the Phillies at the time, wrote, "If the right fielder had eaten onions for lunch, the second baseman knew it."

Although the wall was 40 feet high, fly balls flew over it and landed in the adjacent Broad Street with unrelenting frequency. Often car windshields were broken. The Phillies had a standing policy: Anyone who gets a broken windshield would be reimbursed by the club.

Right fielder Chuck Klein was aided by the right-field dimensions on two fronts, especially during the 1930 season. First, his record 44 outfield assists were greatly enhanced by the shallowness of right field in relation to the infield. Second, his home-run hitting prowess was aided by the short right field, and he hit 26 of his 40 home runs in 1930 at home. In fact, Klein slapped so many balls over the wall that owner William Baker had a 20-foot-high screen added to the top of the wall, bringing

Outfield wall and scoreboard, Baker Bowl

Outfield wall and old scoreboard, Shibe Park, 1951

Outfield wall and scoreboard, Shibe Park, 1960s

Outfield wall and scoreboards, Veterans Stadium, 2001

Liberty Bell sign being removed from Veterans Stadium, February 2004

the total height to 60 feet. "Home runs have become too cheap at the Philadelphia ballpark," Baker said. Some speculated that Baker was afraid Klein might start to demand a higher salary, so he had to be kept in check.

For many years, a huge Lifebuoy sign hung on the right-center field part of the wall. "The Phillies use Lifebuoy," the sign proclaimed. "And they still stink," some wag had, at one point, scribbled on the sign.

The right-field wall at Shibe Park/Connie Mack Stadium was almost as notorious. The distance down the right-field line from home plate varied over the years between 340 and 329 feet, while ranging from 378 to 312 feet in left and from 515 to 410 feet in center.

Originally, the wall that stretched from right to center field was 12 feet high, and fans would sit on the rooftops of row houses across the street to watch games for free. Realizing that he was missing out on a substantial amount of ticket revenue, Connie Mack had 22 feet of wall added, thereby blocking the views of the rooftop watchers—and also severely reducing the number of home runs hit to right field. Unhappy neighbors called it the "Spite Wall" and took Mack to court but lost the case.

Like the much smaller one at Baker Bowl, a scoreboard also sat in right-center field at Shibe Park. The first one was about 30 feet high and was mostly devoted to providing out-of-town scores. In 1956, the Phillies replaced it with a 50-foot-high scoreboard that had a 10-foot-high Ballantine Beer sign above it, and a 15-foot-high Longines clock sitting atop that. Considerably more informative than its predecessor, it was actually a used scoreboard that had been in Yankee Stadium. Purchased for $175,000 after the Yankees bought themselves a new one, the scoreboard was dismantled and trucked to Philadelphia.

In later years, the lower parts of both walls were covered with advertisements. There were also advertisements atop the left-field roof. Occasionally, power hitters such as Jimmie Foxx and Dick

Outfield wall and scoreboards, Citizens Bank Park, 2009

Allen hit balls over the roof. Once, an Allen blast that cleared not only the roof but a row of houses behind was measured as having traveled 529 feet.

Just like its forebears, Veterans Stadium was a hitter-friendly park, with balls flying into the seats more often than in most arenas. The stands stood a highly reachable 330 feet down both foul lines and 408 to center, with an 8-foot-high wall surrounding the outfield. During the first season, the wall was raised to 12 feet.

One of the most conspicuous features at the Vet was a 4,000-pound steel replica of the Liberty Bell, which sat above the roof of the upper deck in center field. Later relocated to the façade at the 400 level, it was once hit by a 500-foot clout off the bat of Greg Luzinski.

The Vet also introduced a scoreboard phenomenon called Phanovision. Two computerized screens, each measuring 100 by 25 feet, weighing 66 tons apiece, and costing $4 million, were mounted on the right and left-center field walls. Two other 90-by 13-foot auxiliary scoreboards were located between the upper and lower decks, and a square screen that showed pictures and statistics hung on the façade near the Liberty Bell.

Unlike the symmetrical Vet, the wall around the outfield at Citizens Bank Park has varying distances and heights. The wall stands 329 feet down the left-field line, 401 to center, and 330 to right. Between left and center fields, the wall is angled in such a way that it has recesses and crannies that range from 369 to 409 feet from home. The stadium developed a reputation soon after it opened as one of the most hitter-friendly parks in baseball. Early in its life, CBP was yielding so many home runs to left-center that three rows of seats were removed, and the wall was moved back.

The park also features some of the best scoreboards in baseball. A massive scoreboard above the left-field stands shows pictures of the batters and keeps fans up-to-date on lineups and statistics. Smaller scoreboards providing a variety of other information, such as the pitch counts of every hurler, are placed at lower levels in right and right-center and between the second and third decks down the third-base line.

One of the Cit's most notable accoutrements is a 35- by 50-foot Liberty Bell that hangs 100 feet above street level. With a variety of different-colored lights, it flashes and sways back and forth whenever a Phillies player hits a home run. All the while, a clanging sound blares out of the loudspeakers. Ryan Howard, with blasts that occasionally reach the third level, has been ringing the ball steadily for the last five seasons. Chase Utley, Jimmy Rollins, Raul Ibañez, and Jayson Werth have also given the bell plenty of action, as did Pat Burrell.

Fans lining up to enter Baker Bowl, circa 1930s

UP IN THE STANDS

Phillies fans are among the most knowledgeable and avid fans in the land, and they've never had any reservations about making that point obvious. This is a group that doesn't hesitate to vent its feelings. A Phillies player makes a crucial mistake or doesn't hustle? He gets booed. He goes all-out? He could run for mayor and win. Cheers and boos—they're both exercised with frequency and at the utmost discretion.

Booing has always been a staple of Philadelphia fandom. Fans once threw snowballs at Santa Claus at an Eagles game. "I've seen people standing on street corners booing each other," said that noted comedian, announcer, and former Phillies catcher Bob Uecker. "The fans are so rough," he added, "that they boo kids who come up empty at an Easter egg hunt. One time, a guy fell out of the stands, and the crowd booed when he tried to get up."

In the midst of the 1980 season, shortstop Larry Bowa described Phillies fans as "front runners" who are "the worst in baseball." About a month later, after the Phillies' World Series victory parade, Bowa said, "This is the greatest moment in my life, and I'm glad I can share it with the greatest fans in baseball."

Phillies fans love a winner and despise a loser. The only thing they dislike more is the visiting team, especially if it's the New York Mets or, in earlier times, the Brooklyn Dodgers.

Since they moved into Citizens Bank Park in 2004, Phillies fans have become more numerous. The Phils drew three million fans in a season only once (1980) before that. In the first six years at the new ballpark, the team drew three million in attendance four times, including an all-time record 3,600,693 in 2009, when more than 70 of the team's home games were sellouts.

Overall, the crowd is a little more refined, as might be expected when good seats sell for $30 and up. It has become the "in" thing to attend a Phillies game, and fans of all ages pack the stands, not to mention all the eateries and other side attractions that clutter the stadium. Families and bands of 20- and 30-somethings, who have taken a page from football tradition and set up pre-game tailgate parties in the parking lots, seem to be the most conspicuous attendees.

In general, though, the fans (most of whom come to the games wearing red) really haven't toned down their act all that much from the days of old. Philly's famous boobirds, who at times have made players such as Del Ennis, Dick Allen, Mike Schmidt, and Pat Burrell special targets, are still alive. There is little tolerance for bad calls by umpires or bad plays by the home team. And the beer still flows, the hecklers still heckle, an occasional fight still breaks out in the stands, and the noise level can be positively deafening, especially if the Phillies just did something good.

Such traits have been in existence since baseball began in Philadelphia. In a city known for its savvy fans, Philly has always been a place where the paying customers were on top of the action. No casual, sleepy-eyed, leave-in-the-seventh-inning fans are these. Phils fans know exactly what is going on, and they react accordingly.

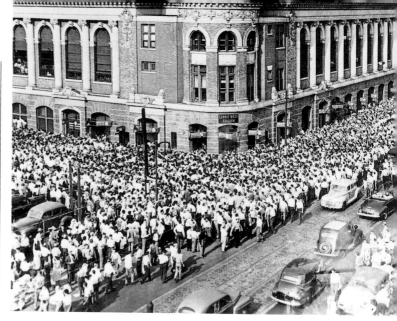

Fans lining up to enter Connie Mack Stadium, 1950s

Fans entering Citizens Bank Park, 2008

Bleachers, Baker Bowl, 1915

Sparse crowd at Shibe Park, 1940s

Full crowd on Bat Day, Connie Mack Stadium, 1967

In earlier days when the Phillies called Baker Bowl their home and 50 cents could buy a good seat, fans were mostly men and boys. Men often came to the ballpark dressed in coats and ties, many wearing hats. Few women and even fewer African Americans attended games.

Over the years when the Phils played horrendously, there were often as few as 1,000 in the stands. Many of them were gamblers, some of whom bet on every pitch. A good year at the gate seldom drew more than 300,000 for the season, and often

yearly crowds fell well below 200,000. In 1933, the Phils drew 156,421 for the entire season.

Baker Bowl fans were first-rate hecklers. Often, when they disagreed with something that happened, they'd throw seat cushions, rented because the hard, wooden seats were so uncomfortable, onto the field. Sometimes, those in the upper deck would stomp on the floor so hard that rusty metal fragments would drop on the spectators below. Frequently, the largest number of fans sat in bleachers that lined the left- and right-field

Fans at World Series Game Five, Citizens Bank Park, October 2008

foul lines and from left to center field. In the 1930s, those seats cost 50 cents, while a box seat went for $1.65, and a grandstand seat could be had for $1.10

At Shibe Park, later to be called Connie Mack Stadium, fans continued to exhibit their passion for baseball. After the Phils began playing respectably, crowds started getting bigger. The first year the Phillies passed one million in attendance was in 1946. Four years later when they won their first pennant in 35 years, the Phils drew more than 1.2 million, all of whom had the pleasure of sitting in metal seats with armrests. In the 1940s and 1950s, a grandstand seat could be purchased for $1.50 and a reserved seat for $3.00.

As before, the fans knew the game in and out, they loved the home team when things went well, and they could raise a ruckus as well as anybody in baseball. Such was the case during a game in 1949 when fans peppered the field with so many bottles and other items in protest of an umpire's call that the game had to be forfeited to the visiting New York Giants.

After Veterans Stadium opened in 1971, crowds increased significantly. In 1993, when the team went to the World Series, the Phillies passed three million in attendance for the first time. Thirteen other times attendance went over two million. Special promotions helped to draw big crowds.

Vet spectators, who sat in comfortable plastic seats with prices originally being $1.75 for the grandstand and $4.00 for a reserved seat, were generally younger than earlier Phils fans. And they were close followers of the better players. A favored player received exceptionally loyal treatment and was given much more latitude in his performance. The boobirds, of course, were still there. So were the other rowdies. Many fans complained loudly in later years about conditions at the Vet. But, as always, Phillies fans remained among the most lively, smart, and enthusiastic in baseball.

Since grandpa went to his first baseball game many decades ago, there have been numerous significant changes in the kinds of reading material that a team puts out about itself. Grandpa might have bought a program, but he didn't get a yearbook because they hadn't been invented yet. And if he happened to be a sportswriter, there was no such thing as a media guide.

Nowadays, even in the age of electronic gadgetry, paper products such as programs, yearbooks, and media guides can be found everywhere. Collectively, they provide stories and information that describe virtually every conceivable fact and figure about the team, some of which can't even be found on the internet.

Originally called scorecards, the Phillies issued game programs as early as 1883 and on into the 1900s. By then, the scorecard was a piece of cardboard divided into four pages that cost five cents. It included a front-page picture, a printed lineup and blanks for scoring, a schedule of home games, and numerous small advertisements.

Eventually, the product was expanded and called a program. It stayed the same size for many years, but by 1948 it

was 16 pages of thin paper and cost 10 cents. Articles by local writers, rosters, and other material had been added.

The programs varied in price, size, and thickness in the ensuing years, with magazine-size publications offered from the 1960s on. By the 1990s, a program could be 96 pages thick, cost $2, and contain color photos, feature articles, player profiles, schedules of every team, and advertisements galore. Still later, programs stretched well over 100 pages, cost $10, and—unlike the older programs that were somewhat modified for every game—were issued as entirely new publications six times a season.

Yearbooks, meanwhile, were changing just as much. The first Phillies yearbook was published in 1949, sold for 50 cents, and contained 40 pages, consisting mostly of profiles on team personnel, team records, a little bit of history, a few feature articles, and plenty of ads. Except for a brief interlude in 1950 and 1951 when the yearbook was printed in digest size—the price on the Whiz

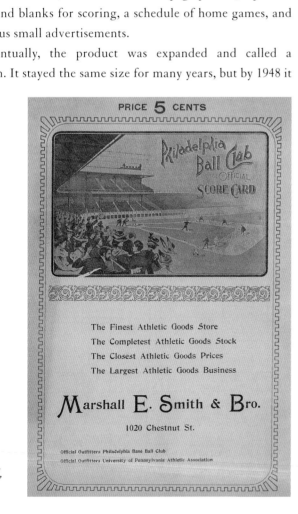

Phillies scorecard, 1900

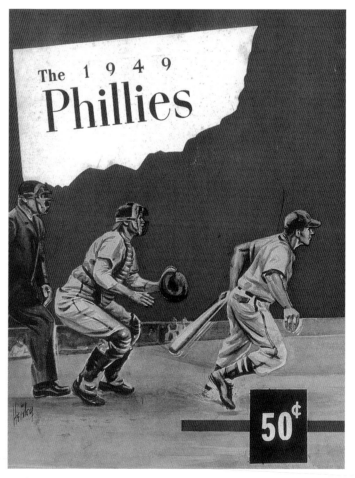

Phillies yearbook, 1949

Kids yearbook dropped curiously to 25 cents—the publication remained essentially the same in the decades ahead, with the price increasing to $1 in 1959. In some years, second editions were printed if there had been a major change in the roster.

As the years went on, yearbooks, like the team's programs and media guides, became considerably more professional in both design and content, with the editorial and photographic material becoming bigger, better, and more attractive. By the 1980s, the price stretched to $3 and was headed for $10 by 2000. The publication was also getting bigger, and by 2009 it was 152 pages.

It was a similar story with media guides. Although other teams already had media guides, the first Phillies guide was produced in 1964. Public relations director Larry Shenk wrote the entire book, mimeographed 58 pages, and collated them,

then his wife Julie drew and colored each cover. There were no pictures, and only 300 copies were produced.

The following year, a printed guide was published, and while originally just four inches wide and nine inches tall, it grew from 48 pages to 288 by the 1990s. Unlike the early guides that contained mostly information about the current team, later ones offered extensive material on all aspects of the club, past, present, and future.

A major change in size occurred in 1998 when the guide went to 6 by 9 inches. Although that size remains today, the thickness of the publication has increased tremendously. The Phillies' 2009 media guide is 416 pages. More than one dozen members of the front-office staff take part in producing it, and thousands are printed to accommodate media members throughout the country.

Phillies media guide, 1978

Phillies yearbook, 2008

Philadelphia Phillies donning 1876-style uniforms for 60th anniversary of the National League, August 1936

UNIFORMS

One of Al Reach's first chores when he launched his new baseball team in Philadelphia in 1883 was to decide what nickname to use. For Reach, the decision was easy. The team would be called the Phillies.

The name Phillies, Reach reasoned, would easily identify the team with its city. There were some who wanted to call the team the Quakers, but Reach prevailed. As baseball historian Fred Lieb wrote many years later, it "was one of the most natural and spontaneous of all big league nicknames. Any oaf could recognize a Phillie as a player from Philadelphia."

Now, after more than 125 years, the name is the longest, continuous, one-city nickname in professional sports. During much of that time, the word "Phillies" has been emblazoned on the fronts of the team's uniforms. The words first began to appear in the mid-1930s and have in one form or another been shown in most years since then.

There have, of course, been some exceptions. For a few years in the late 1800s, "PHILA" ran across the chests. Before "Phillies" became a fixture, and even as late as the 1970s and 1980s, various forms of the letter *P* were written across the fronts of the team's shirts.

Philadelphia Phillies team portrait, 1889

For a period in the early 1930s, the uniform shirts were blank across the front with the letter "P" placed on both sleeves. Then, in 1942, manager Hans Lobert tried to change the team name from Phillies to Phils because he thought the former had a negative connotation after so many losing seasons. Lobert even had the letters *PHILS* placed on uniforms. As had an earlier attempt to change the name of the team to the Live Wires, Lobert's idea failed to materialize.

Also failing was the plan in 1945 by team president Bob Carpenter to change the name of the team to the Blue Jays. Carpenter put a Blue Jays logo on the sleeves of the team's jerseys, but the bird was gone by the following season.

While the logo and name has seem minimal changes over the years, the styles and materials of the uniforms have gone through numerous variations of their own—from button-down shirts (with collars) to zipper-fronts to pullover jerseys and back to button-downs; from belts to elastic waistbands and back to belts; from wool and flannel-cotton to polyester.

The wool uniforms were, not surprisingly, heavy, hot, and uncomfortable. "You felt like you were wearing a horse blanket," pitcher Bucky Walters once said.

The color scheme of Phillies home uniforms stabilized in about 1950, when the team came out with shirts and pants that featured bright-red pinstripes. The new design was certainly timely. That year, the team won its first pennant since 1915.

The red pinstripes, with red stockings and red-sleeved sweatshirts, have been a fixture of home uniforms for six decades. Gray has been the familiar look when the Phils have played on the road for much of its history, with some departures.

The lightweight, polyester uniforms took on some interesting hues in the 1970s and 1980s, most notably powder blue and, for a brief period, maroon. Ankle-length pant legs have long dominated the team's attire, and on some players today, the red stockings are clearly visible, while others pull the pantlegs below the ankle. And unlike players of old who used to box their hats, current players wear caps of all sizes and shapes, many of them rounded across the top.

Since the Phils began, they have worn at least 12 different kinds of hats. The hats have come in various colors, although over the years, red has been the predominant color. In almost all the years except the earliest, some version of the letter *P* has appeared on the cap. In recent times, the Phils can be seen most often wearing red caps with the white *P* or blue caps with a red *P* and a red bill. The latter is worn at home day games.

Philadelphia Phillies team portrait, 1950

Dode Paskert, circa 1911

Cy Williams, circa 1927

*Jimmie
Wilson,
1934*

Heinie Mueller, late 1930s

Jim Bunning, mid 1960s

Garry Maddox, late 1970s

Steve Carlton, 1980

Chase Utley, 2009

"There's a long drive. Deep left field. Way back. Watch that baby go. . . . It's outta heeeere. Home run, Michael Jack Schmidt."

The call is deeply imbedded in the annals of Philadelphia broadcasting history. And whether it was Mike Schmidt, Ryan Howard, or somebody else hitting one out of the park, there isn't a baseball fan in the region who's not familiar with Harry Kalas' legendary call of a Phillies home run.

It was all part of the aura that surrounded the Phillies' longtime and hugely popular play-by-play announcer. In a city that over the years has built an impressive list of high-level sports broadcasters, Kalas is at the top. He is truly the king of the airwaves in Philadelphia sports.

Kalas' success was not based on just his calls, however. It was his golden voice; his positive, down-to-earth manner; his cheerful interaction with fans. He was a favorite of the players, and he was one of the most visible sports figures in the region.

A big-league broadcaster for 43 years, the Chicago-born Kalas started with the Houston Astros in 1965 before joining the Phillies in 1971. He was with the club until his death in 2009 at the age of 73. During his 38 years in Philadelphia, Kalas called countless memorable moments while winning legions of awards for his broadcasting skills.

Harry the K is one of two longtime Phillies announcers enshrined in the broadcasters' wing of the Hall of Fame at Cooperstown. He was inducted in 2002.

Byrum Saam won Cooperstown's Ford C. Frick Award in 1990. The Texas native, a legendary play-caller in his own right, worked Phillies games from 1938 to 1975, developing a large following that was sometimes entertained by his occasionally jumbled pronouncements. A broadcaster of national repute, his trademark phrase was "right you are," and he used that and other memorable lines during his long career, which also included broadcasting Philadelphia Athletics games.

Harry Kalas, 1992

Richie Ashburn (left) and Harry Kalas with manager Paul Owens, after 1983 NLCS

Chris Wheeler (right) with manager Charlie Manuel, after clinching East Division, 2007

Among the Phillies' other noteworthy announcers was former star center fielder Richie Ashburn. One of the most popular figures in Philadelphia sports history, the Nebraska native began in the booth in 1963, shortly after the end of his playing career. He handled the color commentary until his sudden passing in 1997, two years after his election to the Hall of Fame as a player.

Bill Campbell was another well-known announcer, working with the club from 1963 to 1970. Still active after more than 60 years behind the mike, Campbell not only called Phillies games, but also Philadelphia Eagles and Warriors games. Owner of one of the most melodious voices on the air, Campbell was one of the few Philadelphia natives to call Phillies games.

Another local from suburban Philadelphia is Chris Wheeler. In 1977, Wheeler entered the broadcasting booth while still serving in the club's public relations department. Ultimately, "Wheels" moved into broadcasting full time. Over the years, his astute observations and distinct knowledge of baseball have given him a special place on the Phils' broadcasting team.

Andy Musser, a Harrisburg native, worked behind the mike as the play-by-play man from 1976 until 2001, while also broadcasting other Philadelphia sports for much of that time.

Gene Kelly also stands on the pedestal of top Phillies announcers; his distinct style was heard from 1950 to 1959.

The Phillies participated in baseball's first broadcasted game on August 5, 1921, when station KDKA in Pittsburgh aired a contest between the Phils and Pirates. The team broadcast a few of its own games in 1928 and 1929 and then began a full-time home schedule in 1936. The team first appeared in a televised game in 1941.

Chuck Thompson, who went on to an outstanding career with the Baltimore Orioles, spent two years in the Phillies booth. Herb Carneal, longtime voice of the Minnesota Twins, worked one year in Philadelphia. Both are enshrined in Cooperstown.

Along the way, numerous ex-Phillies have helped to call games on radio and television. Larry Andersen has spent 12 years in the booth. Other players-turned-broadcasters over the years include Robin Roberts, Tim McCarver, Garry Maddox, Mike Schmidt, Kent Tekulve, Jay Johnstone, John Kruk, and Gary Matthews. Manager Jim Fregosi also spent a year behind the mike.

Wheeler, Andersen, and Matthews, along with play-by-play announcers Scott Franzke and Tom McCarthy, constituted the Phillies broadcasting team in 2009.

Byrum Saam, late 1940s

Gene Kelly, 1950s

Spring Training

When the Phillies held spring training in Clearwater, Florida, for the first time in 1947, no one would've dared to predict that more than six decades later, the team would still be there. After all, before then, the Phils had conducted preseason drills at no fewer than 20 different locations since 1899. Many times, they spent one spring at a site, never to return.

The Phillies have come a long way from their first spring training. In the maiden season of 1883, the team trained at Recreation Park, the Phils' regular-season home at the time. The first exhibition game was against the Ashland Club, a semipro team from nearby Manayunk. Phils pitcher John Coleman, who would go on to lose 48 games that season, threw a no-hitter.

Recreation Park continued as the spring training site for a number of years. Eventually, the Phillies went south, at one point traveling as far as Jacksonville, Florida. Then in 1900, manager Billy Shettsline decided that the team needed to seek a warm climate for preseason preparation on a regular basis, and he took the Phils to Charlotte, North Carolina. In one exhibition game there, the Phillies defeated St. Mary's College, 11–6. Afterward, the Philadelphia *Evening Bulletin* reported that the vastly overweight Shettsline was so happy that on the way back to the hotel, "he fell out of the carriage" into a pool of mud.

The Phillies were one of the first major-league teams to travel south consistently for spring training. But after one spring in Charlotte, they embarked on a seemingly endless odyssey through the South, which included stops in Richmond, Virginia; Savannah and Augusta, Georgia; Birmingham, Alabama; Hot Springs, Arkansas; Wilmington, North Carolina; Biloxi, Mississippi; New Braunfels, Texas; and St. Petersburg, Bradenton, Winter Haven, and Miami, Florida.

During World War II, teams were required by the federal government to hold spring training close to home. The Phillies practiced one year in Hershey, Pennsylvania, and two years in Wilmington, Delaware.

Following the vagabond approach of the first half of the twentieth century, the Phillies finally settled in at Clearwater as their permanent spring home. After completing their 64th year there, in 2010, the club has spent spring training in one city longer than any team in baseball except the Detroit Tigers, who have been going to Lakewood, Florida, every spring since 1934.

Chuck Klein stretching, with Claude Passeau during spring training at New Braunfels, Texas, 1939

Mike Schmidt and Jay Johnstone stretching during spring training at Jack Russell Stadium, Clearwater, Florida, 1977

Cole Hamels (left) stretching during spring training at the Carpenter Complex, Clearwater, Florida, 2009

During their years in Clearwater, the Phillies have seen the town grow from a sleepy fishing village with 15,000 residents to a full-fledged metropolis with a year-round population of 100,000, which doubles in the winter. Team personnel have gone from all staying at what was the only hotel in town—the Fort Harrison Hotel—to living in condos and rented houses along nearby beaches.

Initially, spring training in Clearwater was held at a rundown little wooden ballpark called Athletic Field, which had previously been used by the Cleveland Indians and Brooklyn Dodgers. The ballpark was not big-league caliber, however, and another site was needed. Fortunately for the Phillies, they were not alone in that view.

Local resident Jack Russell had pitched in the majors for 15 years with the Chicago Cubs and Washington Senators. A Texan by birth, he had settled in Clearwater after his playing days ended and in time became owner of an oil business and a city commissioner.

Russell pushed hard for a new ballpark, and his work paid off. A new stadium opened in 1955. As a tribute to the driving force behind its construction, the park was named Jack Russell Stadium.

In the late 1980s, the Phillies added a new facility called Carpenter Complex. A few miles from Jack Russell, it had four practice diamonds and a large clubhouse, and it was used by both the Phils and their minor league clubs.

The Phillies played at Jack Russell through 2003. The following year, Bright House Field, located next to Carpenter Complex, was opened. A sparkling venue with all the trimmings and a seating capacity of 7,300, the park ranks as one of Florida's top Grapefruit League sites. At times, crowds of as many as 10,000 have jammed the park to enjoy its comfortable seating, stellar sight lines, sloping outfield berm, and closeness to the playing field. Behind the scenes, well-appointed clubhouses and side rooms, media facilities, and club offices add to the first-class stature of the attractive ballpark.

Phillies spring training at Coffee Pot Park, St. Petersburg, Florida, 1915

Phillies spring training game at Bright House Field, Clearwater, Florida, 2009

Reading Municipal Memorial Stadium (now FirstEnergy Stadium), home of the Reading Phillies

THE FARM SYSTEM

Stability has not been a strong suit of the Phillies farm system. Since 1944, the Phillies have had minor league teams in 83 different cities, only 7 of which housed the Phillies affiliate for more than 10 consecutive years.

The granddaddy of all Phillies minor league cities is Reading. The Phils have been operating a farm team there since 1967. A member of the Class AA Eastern League, the Reading Phillies have been a stopping point for virtually every player who has come to the parent club through its farm system for more than four decades.

Of all the other farm teams, only those in Batavia, New York (1988–2006); Bradford, New York (1944–1955); Clearwater, Florida (1986–2010); Martinsville, Virginia (1988–1999); Scranton/Wilkes-Barre, Pennsylvania (1989–2007); and Spartanburg, South Carolina (1963–1994) have lasted in the Phillies' system for more than one decade.

Among the other cities that have played host to minor league affiliates over the years are Baltimore; Buffalo; Dallas; Indianapolis; Little Rock; Portland, Oregon; San Diego; and Syracuse. In several cases, such as Chattanooga; Eugene, Oregon; Miami; Hampton, Virginia; Portland, Maine; and Schenectady, the Phils have underwritten teams, pulled out, then returned with a team at a different level. Hampton was home to the Peninsula Phillies in 1970 and 1971, and they returned as the Peninsula Pilots from 1976 to 1985.

The Phillies have had connections to varying degrees with minor league teams dating back to 1932, when they had a working agreement with the Class B Piedmont League's Durham Bulls, then managed by former Phils outfielder George "Possum" Whitted. At various times after that, the major league organization had loose arrangements with teams in Trenton, Hazleton, and Utica.

Left: *War Memorial Stadium, Hampton, Virginia*

The number of affiliates began to increase in the mid-1940s when the Carpenter family bought the club and Hall of Fame pitcher Herb Pennock became the general manager. With Joe Reardon serving as the club's first minor league director, the Phillies signed working agreements with 15 minor league franchises in 1948, including the International League's Toronto Maple Leafs, the Interstate League's Wilmington Blue Rocks, and the Carbondale Pioneers of the North Atlantic League, one of 25 Class D leagues then in existence.

Since the 1950s, the number of affiliates has declined, and today the Phillies have five full-season farm teams: the Lehigh Valley Iron Pigs, Reading Phillies, Clearwater Threshers, Lakewood Blue Claws, and Williamsport Crosscutters. The Phils also operate three short-season clubs, including two in Latin America. The Gulf Coast League Phillies at the rookie level play at the big league club's spring training Carpenter Complex in Clearwater, Florida.

Since the job was created, the organization has had just 12 farm directors, starting with Reardon (1943–1954). The most celebrated minor league honcho was Paul Owens, who took over an ailing system and between 1965 and 1972 built it into one of the best in the majors. Dallas Green picked up where Owens left off, serving in the job for 8 years (1972–1979). Del Unser (1989–1998) held the post for 10 years. He was followed by Mike Arbuckle

Lackawanna County Stadium (now PNC Field), home of the Scranton/Wilkes-Barre Red Barons

(1999–2008), who is credited with putting together the farm system that was a major contributing factor in producing a World Championship team in Philadelphia in 2008.

Phillies farm teams have won 44 league championships, with Class A Spartanburg contributing 6 of them. Danny Carnevale and Skeeter Newsome each managed four titlists, while Lucchesi and Bill Dancy each skippered three winners.

Photo and Illustration Credits

We wish to acknowledge the following for providing the illustrations included in the book. Every effort has been made to locate the copyright holders for materials used, and we apologize for any oversights. Unless otherwise noted, all other images are from the author's collection. Individual photographers and collections are listed for photographs when known.

AP/Wide World Photos: p. 9 bottom (Chris Carlson); 10; 11 top (Ron Frehm); 13 right (Rusty Kennedy); 22 left; 24 (David Zalubowski); 27 left; 29 top (H. Rumph Jr.); 29 bottom (Larry Stoddard); 32 (Rusty Kennedy); 35 top (Bill Ingraham); 35 bottom (Bradley C. Bower); 40 top (Chris Gardner); 40 bottom (Tom Mihalek); 41 left (George Widman); 51 right; 61 left (Chris Gardner); 71 (Tom Mihalek); 75 top; 87 bottom (Gene Puskar); 88 right; 89 left; 98 (Bill Haber); 99 left (Tom Gannam); 101 left (Kolenovsky); 105 top; 105 bottom (Peter Morgan); 109 bottom (Julia Robertson); 111; 115 top (Rusty Kennedy); 115 bottom (George Widman); 119 top; 120 bottom (George Widman); 136 (Gene Puskar).

Getty Images: p. 2 (Rob Tringali/Sportschrome); 7 (Joe Robbins); 11 bottom (Jim McIsaac); 14 (Doug Benc); 15 left (Walter Iooss Jr./*Sports Illustrated*); 15 right (Elsa); 16 top (Andy Hayt/*Sports Illustrated*); 17 left (Heinz Kluetmeier/ *Sports Illustrated*); 17 right (Tom Mihalek/AFP); 18 (Elsa); 19 (Al Tielemans/*Sports Illustrated*); 23 (Chris Gardner); 24 (David Zalubowski); 26 bottom (Walter Iooss Jr./*Sports Illustrated*); 27 right (MLB Photos); 31 right (Hunter Martin); 33 top (Rogers Photo Archive); 33 bottom (Tom Mihalek/AFP); 39 top (Robert Morse/Time Life Pictures); 41 right (Pool); 44 (Drew Hallowell); 47 right (Ezra Shaw); 49 left (Rogers Photo Archive); 52 left (Focus on Sport); 52 right (Stephen Dunn); 53 left (Doug Pensinger); 53 right (Joe Robins); 56 left (Focus on Sport); 56 right (Tim DeFrisco/ Allsport); 57 (Rob Tringali/Sportschrome); 60 left (Focus on Sport); 61 right (Stephen Dunn); 61 right (Hunter Martin); 63 right (Elior Elisofon/Time Life Pictures); 64 top and bottom (Walter Iooss Jr./*Sports Illustrated*); 65 left (Mitchell Layton); 65 right (Rob Tringali/Sportschrome); 69 top (Richard Mackson/*Sports Illustrated*); 69 bottom (Hunter Martin); 73 right (Walter Iooss Jr./*Sports Illustrated*); 74 (Darryl Norenberg/WireImage); 75 bottom (Jed Jacobsohn); 78 (Focus on Sport); 79 top (Rich Pilling/ MLB Photos); 79 bottom (Al Tielemans/*Sports Illustrated*); 80 right (Rogers Photo Archive); 82 right (Focus on Sport); 83 left (Mitchell Layton); 83 right (Joe Robbins); 84 right (Rick Stewart/Allsport); 85 (G. Fiume); 89 right (Jeff Zelevansky); 91 (Rich Pilling/MLB Photos); 93 left (Hulton Archive); 94 bottom (Focus on Sport); 95 left (Al Tielemans/*Sports Illustrated*); 95 right (Scott Cunningham); 99 right (Rich Pilling/MLB Photos); 100 right (Focus on Sport); 101 right (Mike Ehrmann); 103 (Rick Stewart); 104 bottom (Focus on Sport); 107 top (Al Bello/Allsport); 107 bottom (Mark Cunningham); 109 top (MLB Photos); 112 (Doug Pensinger/Allsport); 113 (Nick Laham); 116 top right (Focus on Sport); 116 bottom (Doug Pensinger); 117 (Nick Laham); 120 top (Tom Mihalek/AFP); 121 (Ezra Shaw); 123 bottom (Rich Pilling/MLB Photos); 125 (Doug Pensinger); 131 top left (Photofile/MLB Photos); 131 bottom left (Heinz Kluetmeier/*Sports Illustrated*); 131 bottom right (Rob Tringali/Sportschrome); 132 (David E. Klutho/*Sports Illustrated*); 133 bottom (Al Tielemans/*Sports Illustrated*); 135 right (Walter Iooss Jr./*Sports Illustrated*); 137 bottom (J. Mer).

Library of Congress, Prints and Photographs Division: p. 6; 8; 12 (Bain Collection); 14 top (Bain Collection); 12 top; 30 left; 30 right (Bain Collection); 45 left; 50 right (Bain Collection); 66 (Bain Colelction); 72 right (Bain Collection); 76 right (Bain Collection); 88 left; 90 left (Bain Collection); 92 left; 92 right (Bain Collection); 116 top left (Bain Collection); 124 top left); 130 top left (Bain Collection).

National Baseball Hall of Fame Library, Cooperstown, N.Y.: p. 34; 47 left; 55 right; 67 left; 70 left; 77 top and bottom; 80 left; 100 left; 118; 122; 124 bottom left; 130 top right and bottom left; 131 top right.

Transcendental Graphics/The Rucker Archive: p. 9 top; 20; 25 left; 31 left; 50 left; 62 left; 81; 90 right; 94 top; 102 left; 104 top; 106; 110 bottom; 128 bottom.

INDEX

ABOUT THE AUTHOR

Rich Westcott has served on the staffs of various newspapers and magazines in the Philadelphia area during more than 40 years as a writer and editor.

Westcott is the author of 19 previous books, including *The Fightin' Phils: Oddities, Insights, and Untold Stories*; *The Phillies Encyclopedia* (with Frank Bilovsky), a local best-seller now in its third edition; *Tales from the Phillies Dugout*; *Phillies '93: An Incredible Season*; *Philadelphia's Old Ballparks*; *A Century of Philadelphia Sports*; and *Veterans Stadium: Field of Memories*. Westcott also wrote the book on local baseball legend Mickey Vernon, entitled *Mickey Vernon: The Gentleman First Baseman*. He has authored three books that are collections of interviews and profiles of some 120 former major league baseball players. Other books include *Great Home Runs of the 20th Century*, *Winningest Pitchers: Baseball's 300-Game Winners*, and *No-Hitters: The 225 Games Between 1893 and 1999*.

Westcott was the founding owner and for 14 years the publisher and editor of *Phillies Report*, a newspaper covering the local major league baseball team. He was also a member of a five-person committee and chief writer assigned to plan and produce the permanent interior historical exhibits displayed at the Phillies' Citizens Bank Park. He has also written for numerous national publications.

Considered the leading authority on Phillies history, Westcott has appeared in seven documentaries, including three produced by Major League Baseball. He is president of the Philadelphia Sports Writers' Association, serves on the selection committee for the Phillies Hall of Fame, and is an advisor to the Philadelphia Sports Hall of Fame. He has also been a journalism instructor at La Salle and Temple Universities. Westcott has been inducted into the Delaware County Athletes Hall of Fame, the 21st Ward (Roxborough) Athletic Association Sports Hall of Fame, and the Pennsylvania Sports Hall of Fame.